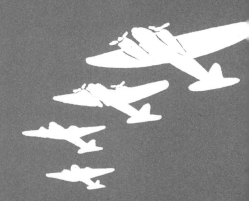

AMAZING AND EXTRAORDINARY FACTS

LONDON AT WAR

LONDON AT WAR

Stephen Halliday

RYDON
PUBLISHING

A Rydon Publishing Book
35 The Quadrant
Hassocks
West Sussex
BN6 8BP
www.rydonpublishing.co.uk
www.rydonpublishing.com

First published by Rydon Publishing in 2016

ISBN: 978-1-910821-08-4

Printed in Poland by BZ Graf

CONTENTS

INTRODUCTION

Since the departure of the Romans in 410 AD, the kingdom of England has only ever had one capital city – and that has always been London.

During the 9th century, Alfred the Great, who subdued Danish invaders and obliged them to confine themselves to the vicinity of East Anglia, did establish his capital at Winchester, but he was King of Wessex, not England. Yet even Alfred recognized the special importance of London, granting the trading post of Aldwych, meaning 'old settlement' in Anglo-Saxon, to the Danes as part of the peace settlement to keep them outside the Roman walls of the City itself. The last king to be crowned in Winchester was Edward the Confessor, his ill-fated successor King Harold being crowned in Westminster in 1066 instead. It is significant that when William the Conqueror triumphed at the Battle of Hastings the same year, he also immediately made his way to Westminster for his coronation.

From that time London has been the political, commercial, financial and cultural capital of England. This combination of activities is unusual amongst capital cities: Washington is the political capital of the USA, but its financial capital is New York; Germany has Berlin and Frankfurt; Italy has Rome and Milan; and China has Beijing and Shanghai. In the Middle Ages, London's leadership in commerce and finance strengthened with its development as the centre of the wool trade in both England and Europe, while during the 18th and 19th centuries London became the world's largest port and its most active centre of finance, insurance and commerce.

The city's importance in all these vital fields has inevitably made London a focus for warfare. King Charles I's abandonment of the capital in 1642 at the beginning of his war with Parliament proved to be his first fatal step along the road to the loss of his throne and his life. In 1694, the Bank of England was founded in London to raise money for wars against King Louis XIV of France. Much of the bank's money was subscribed by Huguenot refugees, who had fled to London after persecution by the French king. They subsequently constructed one of their temples in Threadneedle Street, close to the site of the future bank.

Inevitably, this concentration of politics, trade and wealth in one city has also made London a target for the country's enemies. In World War I, Kaiser Wilhelm II of Germany was urged by his military leaders to authorize attacks on the capital by Zeppelins, and later by Gotha IV bi-plane bombers. He was initially reluctant to do so, as many of his relatives in the royal family, then the House of Saxe-Coburg-Gotha, had their homes there. However he soon recognized that no attack on England could be as damaging as an attack on the heart of her empire, London.

As we shall see, this early experience of a new form of warfare caused great anxiety in the British capital, although its effect was modest compared with the onslaught of the Blitz in World War II. However, it did prompt the government to take steps to defend the capital against future conflicts: the most important of these was the construction of the Chain Home radar installations under the direction of the future Commander-in-Chief of Fighter Command, Sir Hugh Dowding. This meant that by the time World War II began, the Chain extended along the south and east coasts to provide an early warning of attacks. With the support of the Observer Corps, this radar installation was to prove crucial in the defence not only of the capital but also of the entire kingdom.

When the Blitz eventually arrived in September 1940, a year after the outbreak of World War II, London was ready. This volume will explain how, with the aid of these preparations, Londoners lived and died at the centre of World War II, the greatest conflict that the world had ever seen – the capital's ordeal being particularly well recorded on film, in sound and in documents. Yet the capital's experience of violent disturbances arising from conflict goes back many centuries before that, so we should first briefly consider these earlier tribulations.

Stephen Halliday, September 2015

Cousins at war
Roses in Temple Gardens

In 1422 the infant Henry VI succeeded his father, the great warrior Henry V, as King of England – the new king was just nine months old. Besides his age, Henry was also peculiarly unsuited to kingship as he probably suffered from what would now be called bi-polar disorder, which meant that for long periods of time he was incapable of coherent communication. Despite being crowned King of England, and uniquely among English kings also King of France, Henry's incapacity for his new role provoked what Sir Walter Scott first called the Wars of the Roses.

The name of this war was derived from the rose emblems that represented the two factions engaged in the struggle for the throne which had developed between the descendants of Edward III's four surviving sons. Henry VI was descended from John of Gaunt, Duke of Lancaster and third son of King Edward; meanwhile Henry VI's cousin, Richard, Duke of York was descended through his mother from Lionel, the second son of King Edward. As the country sensed Henry's weakness, unrest developed into outright war between the Houses of York and Lancaster, as Henry's cousin Richard challenged his position on the throne.

According to Shakespeare in his play *Henry VI, Part I*, the two contending factions gathered in the gardens of the Temple Church, which serves the Inner and Middle Temple Inns of Court in London. Here they declared their allegiance to one side or the other by plucking either a white rose to represent the House of York, or a red rose to represent the House of Lancaster. In Shakespeare's play, the two factions are represented by Richard Plantagenet, later Duke of York, and John Beaufort, later Duke of Somerset and representative of the Lancastrian cause:

Plantagenet: Let him that is a true-
born gentleman
And stands upon the
honor of his birth,
If he suppose that I have
pleaded truth
From off this brier pluck

a white rose with me.

Beaufort: Let him that is no
          coward nor no flatterer,
          But dare maintain the
          party of the truth,
          Pluck a red rose from off
          this thorn with me.

There is no evidence that this event ever occurred in Temple Gardens or elsewhere. However Sir Walter Scott took it up in his now largely forgotten historical novel entitled *Anne of Geierstein*, or *The Maiden of the Mist* (1829), in which the expression 'Wars of the Roses' was first used, and from there it made its way into history books and legends. And the legend persists: to this day, red and

Tudor rose

white roses respectively represent the counties of Lancashire and Yorkshire, including their county cricket teams.

Essex rebels
*Virgin Queen's favourite
loses his head*

Robert Devereux, 2nd Earl of Essex (1565–1601), was descended from Mary, the sister of Anne Boleyn, and was the stepson of Elizabeth I's favourite courtier, Robert Dudley, 1st Earl of Leicester. Perhaps because of Robert's connection with the family of her mother, Anne Boleyn, and with Robert Dudley, whose death she mourned, the ageing Queen Elizabeth appeared to develop a middle-age crush on the dashing and handsome Essex, whose gift for flattery was formidable. She therefore conferred many honours and privileges upon him.

However Essex became presumptuous and ignored the queen's instruction – for example, by joining Sir Francis Drake's raid on Cadiz in 1589, the year after the failed Armada. His next failure was as Lord Lieutenant of Ireland, when his inability to suppress a rebellion was compounded by his habit of granting knighthoods to his soldiers – a privilege normally reserved to the queen alone. Essex returned to England, again contrary to Elizabeth's instructions, so she ordered that he be confined to his house in London and deprived of some of his income.

Enraged, Essex raised a rebellion against the queen and her advisers, and on 8 February 1601 marched from Essex House in the Strand at the head of a party of followers. He anticipated

that the populace of the City would rise in his support – but they didn't. He found himself instead besieged in Essex House, arrested, tried and then executed, as the last person to be beheaded in the Tower of London. The former site of Essex House is now occupied by Essex Street and Essex Court to the south of the Strand, opposite the Royal Courts of Justice.

SHAKESPEARE AGAIN

As with the Wars of the Roses (see Cousins at War), there is a Shakespearean connection to the Essex rebellion. Two weeks before his unwise attempt to subvert Elizabeth's government in 1601, Robert Devereux, Earl of Essex, and a group of his followers paid the players at the Globe Theatre 40 shillings (several thousands of pounds at today's value) to stage Shakespeare's play **Richard II.** *This contained a scene depicting the deposition of the king, which was tantamount to treason and warned the authorities of what was in store. So when the rebellion began, they were ready for him.*

Elizabeth I

Robert Devereux, Earl of Essex

'The birds have flown'
London turns against Charles I

During the Civil Wars that erupted between King Charles I and Parliament in 17th-century Britain, the opening and closing dramas famously occurred in London. On 4 January 1642, Charles entered the House of Commons, occupied the Speaker's chair and ordered the arrest of five Members of Parliament for treason, believing that they were encouraging the London mob to rise against his authority. The Members were not in the house, famously causing Charles to exclaim that 'the birds have flown'.

The king thus turned to the Speaker, William Lenthall, and asked where they were, to which Lenthall replied, 'May it please your Majesty, I have neither eyes to see nor tongue to speak in this place but as the House is pleased to direct me, whose servant I am here'. Lenthall thereby established the principle that the Speaker is the servant of the House, not the king. From that day to this, no reigning monarch has ever again entered the House of Commons. And from this incident arises the tradition that when the monarch sends Black Rod to summon the Commons on the opening of Parliament each year, the door of the House is slammed in his face.

A few days later Charles left London for Nottingham – London was to remain as the centre of government for the Parliamentary forces throughout the conflict, thus denied to the king. However, not all Londoners were enthusiastic about the war. In August 1643, the Parliamentary General William Waller suppressed a riot by women in protest

Charles I

particular, the Thames watermen negotiated a monopoly on river transport. The final act of the Civil Wars was played out in the capital: Charles I was tried in Westminster Hall for treason then executed on a scaffold in front of the Banqueting Hall in Whitehall on 30 January 1649.

Curious encounter
Wellington and Nelson cross paths

The British Army increased in size from approximately 40,000 at the beginning of the wars against Napoleon to almost a quarter of a million by the end of them in 1815. The inevitable tax increases that were required to support the rising cost of these campaigns severely affected some of the cloth manufacturing areas of Yorkshire and Lancashire, which was further compounded by the loss of some overseas markets. However London was less affected, since much of the taxation was applied to victualing the army and navy, much of which was arranged and financed in the city. Nevertheless, during the Napoleonic Wars London was the scene of one of the strangest

against it with such ferocity that the representative of the Doge of Venice reported that the City authorities were 'vigorous in suppression of dissent'. Since the citizens had helped Waller to raise his forces shortly beforehand, this was not only a cruel but also an ungrateful act on his part.

In the event, London was to remain loyal to Parliament throughout the conflict. Although some of its citizens, notably the Guilds, took advantage of the government's need for their support by gaining concessions – in encounters in history.

On 12 September 1805, six weeks prior to the Battle of Trafalgar, the young Arthur Wellesley, aged 36 and later 1st Duke of Wellington, called at Downing Street to meet the cabinet minister Lord Castlereagh. In the waiting room he met a high-ranking naval officer, whose missing right arm told Wellington he was in the presence of Horatio Nelson. As it turned out, Nelson did not recognize the little known major general, whose feats of arms had hitherto been performed in India. Wellington later gave an account of their meeting: 'He entered at once into conversation with me, if I can call it conversation, for it was almost all on his side and all about himself; and really in a style so vain and silly as to surprise and almost disgust me.'

Indeed, Nelson's vanity was notorious; a former commanding officer, Lord St Vincent, described him as 'a great captain at sea but a foolish little fellow on land'. Nelson left the room for his interview with the cabinet minister, who presumably told him something of Wellington's feats, because when Nelson returned

his attitude was unrecognizable from the earlier encounter. In his account, Wellington added: 'All that I thought a charlatan style had vanished and he talked with good sense and a knowledge of subjects both home and abroad that surprised me equally and more agreeably than the first part of our interview had done. In fact he talked like an officer and a statesman. I don't know that I had a conversation that interested me more.'

The two great commanders were never to meet again. The following day Nelson left Portsmouth for Trafalgar, returning only to be buried

Horatio Nelson

in St Paul's Cathedral where he was joined, almost 50 years later, by Wellington. Later in life Wellington acknowledged that, despite their unfortunate first encounter, Nelson 'was really a very superior person'.

Scathing reports
Russell's despatches from the Crimean War

The Crimean War was fought from 1853 to 1856. The conflict ostensibly arose from a petty dispute between Russia and France over which country should exercise authority over some of the holy locations of Jerusalem, which were ruled at the time by the increasingly feeble Ottoman Empire. In reality, the war was caused by Russia's desire to gain access to the Mediterranean, and the determination of Britain and France that she should do no such thing.

The Crimean War is chiefly remembered for the inadequacy of the political and military leadership, the heroic efforts of Florence Nightingale (1820–1910) to care for injured soldiers, and the charge of the Light Brigade. However it was

in London, at the War Office, that Florence Nightingale first persuaded Sidney Herbert, then Secretary for War, to send her to the Crimea to establish a hospital at Scutari (modern Uskadar) to care for wounded and dying troops.

Less celebrated are the attempts of Mary Seacole, a Jamaican woman of mixed race, to do the same. Lacking Florence Nightingale's connections, her approach to London's War Office was rebuffed. Nevertheless, she later travelled to the Crimea on her own initiative to tend to troops on the front line.

However, the major effect of this campaign in London resulted from the despatches of the Irish-born William Howard Russell (1820–1907). As correspondent for *The Times*, his scathing reports on the war exposed the sufferings of the military, and the incompetence of the political and military hierarchy. Russell's persistence in gathering information from soldiers on the front line caused senior commanders to forbid them any contact with him, but Florence Nightingale reported that it was Russell's accounts of the soldiers' sufferings that led her to the Crimea.

Russell was one of the first reporters to make extensive use of the telegraph to bring accounts of the fighting and its consequences to the prompt attention of readers and politicians. He referred to the inadequacy of supplies for the Russian winter, such as decent food and warm clothing. Also to the total inadequacy of medical facilities, which were mitigated only in part by the 'humane barbarity' of battlefield surgeons.

The impact of Russell's despatches was devastating. Besides provoking the decision to send Florence Nightingale into the theatre of war, they instigated the government's decision to commission Isambard Kingdom Brunel to design a prefabricated hospital for her nurses – which unfortunately arrived too late to be of use. They also led to the abolition of the system whereby army commissions were bought rather than earned on merit. Russell, who was eventually knighted, supported a fund set up in memory of Mary Seacole, the neglected heroine of this war.

Florence Nightingale, having returned from the war a national

Florence Nightingale

heroine, used her celebrity to campaign and raise money for the better training of nurses. This in turn led to the creation of the Florence Nightingale School of Nursing that still flourishes, based at St Thomas's Hospital in London.

BY JINGO!
The Crimean War and its aftermath inspired a song. In the following decade this was to be heard sung raucously in London pubs whenever

the Russians showed an inclination to move too close to the Mediterranean and threaten Britain's interests in the Middle East:

> *We don't want to fight but by Jingo if we do,*
> *We've got the ships, we've got the men, we've got the money too,*
> *We've fought the Bear before, and while we're Britons true,*
> *The Russians shall not have Constantinople.*

Thus did the expression 'By Jingo' become firmly established in the vocabulary of Britain.

Mafeking is relieved
London celebrates military success

The final years of Queen Victoria's reign and the first of her successor's, Edward VII, were disfigured by the Boer War that was fought between 1899 and 1902. This was a struggle between the British population of South Africa and their Dutch fellow-colonialists over supremacy in this wealthy and racially

divided colony, a Boer being Dutch and Afrikaans for farmer, the occupation of most of the Dutch fighters. Interestingly, one of the more conspicuous participants in this conflict was the young Winston Churchill, whose capture by the Boers and subsequent dramatic escape established him as a national figure. He wrote an account of his

Robert Baden-Powell

adventures in *From London to Pretoria via Ladysmith*, which was published in 1900 while the war still continued.

The most famous episode of the war was the Siege of Mafeking, when the small town of that name was besieged for seven months from October 1899. It was defended by about 1,100 British troops of varying quality under the command of Colonel Robert Baden-Powell (1857–1941), and tied down 5,000 Boers, who were thereby unable to mount offensives elsewhere. It is now remembered chiefly for the use that Baden-Powell made of young boys, aged between 12 and 15, to act as messengers and orderlies, thus releasing a further thousand men to man the defences. These boys became the inspiration for the foundation of the Scout movement by Baden-Powell eight years later.

The presence of the press in the town of Mafeking, and their enterprise in smuggling despatches through the Boer lines, meant that the siege became the centre of intense public interest back home in London. On 16 May 1900, a long-awaited relief force arrived to lift the siege. This led to wild rejoicing in London, as the news 'Mafeking has been relieved' reached the streets – riotous crowds waved flags, sang, danced and cheered themselves hoarse for hours on end. At Covent Garden, a performance of the opera *Lohengrin* was halted to announce that Mafeking was relieved, and the audience, which included the future Edward VII, broke into song. Factories and ships in the Thames sounded their sirens and horns, and brass bands struck up 'God Save the Queen' and 'Rule Britannia'.

Baden-Powell was portrayed as the hero of the siege and his reputation was made. Morever, this was the first such celebration of a military success that London had seen, and a precursor of similar scenes that took place at the end of the two subsequent world wars.

FROM BOER TO BRITISH WAR CABINET

Jan Smuts (1870–1950) led a Boer commando against the British in the Boer War. Yet after the peace he became Prime Minister of South

Africa, led South African forces against the Germans in World War I, and served in the British War Cabinet towards the end of that conflict. He was involved in the foundation of the RAF, became a field marshal in the British Army in 1941, and served in the Imperial War Cabinet in World War II under Winston Churchill. Moreover, he was the only person to sign the peace treaties that ended both world wars.

WORLD WAR I

Concealing German spies?

Disused London Underground stations are searched

As World War I approached in August 1914, an article appeared in the magazine *Railway and Travel Monthly* – whose editor, G A Sekon, was not noted for his sense of humour. This piece suggested that German spies, accompanied by stores of explosives, armaments and other such materials, might lie concealed in disused London Underground railway tunnels, ready to be brought into use when hostilities began.

Prompted by public anxiety arising from such reports, the Metropolitan Police searched a number of such sites, including the disused King William Street tube station on the northern side of London Bridge. This had been the original terminus of London's first deep-level line, the City & South London Railway (now the Northern Line), but closed in 1900 when it was bypassed and replaced by Bank station.

As it turned out, no sinister people or substances were found during these searches, although the disused King William Street station went on to be used as an air raid shelter in 1940. The station remains even to this day, now used as a document store beneath St Regis House, which stands above it.

TRAITORS AT THE TOWER
During World War I, 11 enemy spies were imprisoned and executed by firing squad at the Tower of London before being buried in a cemetery at Plaistow in East London. The most

Tower of London

celebrated prisoner to be held at the Tower during this conflict was the Irish patriot Sir Roger Casement: he was tried for treason in connection with the Easter Rising in Dublin against British Rule in 1916 and had his character blackened during his subsequent trial. He was actually executed at Pentonville prison, from where his remains were exhumed in 1965 and reburied in Dublin following a state funeral.

In World War II, Hitler's deputy Rudolf Hess was held at the Tower in May 1941 after his flight to England in an apparent attempt to negotiate with the British government. He was later tried at Nuremberg and imprisoned for life in Berlin's Spandau Prison, where he died in 1987. On

15 August 1941, a German spy named Josef Jakobs, who had been captured shortly after parachuting into England, became the last person to be executed at the Tower. At the end of World War II William Joyce, whose broadcasts as Lord Haw-Haw had made him a hate figure during the early stages of the war, was held at the Tower before being tried at the Old Bailey. He was later executed at Wandsworth prison.

In 1952, the last people actually to be imprisoned at the Tower were the notorious Kray twins, for evading military service.

Don't upset the family
Kaiser holds back the bombing of London

In the early months of World War I no air raids occurred in London, as Kaiser Wilhelm II of Germany had originally forbidden any bombs to be dropped on the city. However, as the war continued, he gradually agreed to harsher measures. In January 1915 the Kaiser approved air raids outside London, but the following month he allowed bombing of the London docks.

The Kaiser extended this to the city east of the Tower of London in May – after all, several of his relatives, the British Royal Family, lived in the *West* End! Thus bombs fell from Zeppelins on the outskirts of the capital for the first time on 31 May 1915, and a plaque in Hackney records the site of the first bomb to fall in a residential area that day. In July, the Kaiser finally allowed unlimited bombing of the British capital.

Wilhelm II

Underground refuges
Londoners take shelter from bombing raids

As World War I continued, in the summer of 1917 a sustained bombing attack was launched on London with six raids in a month. This was to prove trivial compared to the onslaught of World War II, but the London Underground announced that its stations would be available as refuges for those caught in the streets when a bombing raid began. Yet the terror inflicted on the civilian population by this new menace from the air prompted many Londoners to seek shelter in the London Underground in anticipation of raids.

In September 1917, the *Railway Gazette* disapprovingly reported that 'on Monday evening the platforms of the tube railways in all parts of London were crowded with men, women and children', a feature being 'the large number of pet dogs which accompanied their owners into safety'. Some of these refugees moved permanently onto station platforms, while others travelled endlessly round the Circle Line.

Later that month the London Underground introduced a ticketing system for admission to the stations in an attempt to curtail this development – the rule was only relaxed when an air raid warning siren was sounded. On the first evening of the ticketing system the *Railway Gazette* reported a panic at Liverpool Street station among 'people of the poorer class, mostly aliens'.

In February 1918, during a final sequence of raids on the capital, 300,000 people took refuge in the Tube. This number was almost twice that found there during the far worse raids of the Blitz in World War II – although it must be remembered that during the conflict between 1914 and 1918 the provision of air raid shelters was much poorer. Altogether 181 people were killed in London during World War I, less than 1 per cent of the number killed in the later conflict.

SHAMEFUL EPISODE

As World War I progressed German shops, long established in their communities, had their windows broken, and dachshund dogs were kicked off the pavements. Under Parliamentary Privilege the MP Pemberton Billing denounced German-born philanthropist Sir Edgar Speyer, a patron of the early Promenade Concerts and of Scott's Antarctic expeditions, as a traitor. As a result, Speyer offered to resign his baronetcy and Privy Councillorship, both awarded for his services to his adopted country. King George V refused his offer, but Speyer nevertheless left Britain for the USA – a shameful episode.

Preferable to hobbledehoys
Women employed on the London Underground

As World War I gathered pace, the London Underground lost an increasing proportion of its employees to military service, as demonstrated by the fictional character Jack Firebrace of Sebastian Faulks's novel *Birdsong*. Employed in the war effort for his tunnelling skills, Jack burrowed beneath German trenches on the Western Front to blow up the enemy.

Female station staff, London Underground

Gazette sniffily commented that this arrangement was 'preferable to employing hobbledehoys'!

Women were later employed in other Underground duties, such as 'gatemen' on trains – before the advent of sliding doors, each carriage had gates at each end that were opened to admit passengers at stations. Drivers and guards were invariably male – the line had to be drawn somewhere for fear of offending the *Railway Gazette*! – but it was a start. In 2001 Transport for London began to advertise for women to drive trains.

As a result of workforce shortages, and following consultation with the trade unions, in 1915 the London Underground management agreed that women could temporarily replace men for certain duties. Thus on 6 June 1915, Maida Vale station opened on the new Bakerloo Line extension to Queen's Park: this was the first station on the network to be run entirely by female staff, although it shared a male stationmaster with three neighbouring stations. On this occasion the *Railway*

EQUAL PAY – 55 YEARS EARLY

Almost unnoticed, the women who worked on London Underground trains and stations from 1915 were, by agreement with the trade unions, paid the same rates as men – 55 years before Barbara Castle's Equal Pay Act of 1970. This is surprising, but may be explained by the fact that the rail unions did not want the practice of employing women to continue after the war at the expense of men returning from the conflict. If women

had been paid less than men, the
management would have had strong
reasons for increasing the female
labour force, thereby excluding men
and driving down wages.

Wearing the trousers
Women employed in industry
and services

It was not only on the London
Underground that women found
themselves performing traditionally
male jobs (see Preferable to
Hobbledehoys). By the end of World
War I, the British transport network
employed approximately 50,000
women as ticket collectors, bus
conductors and porters.

However, by far the greatest use
of women was in munitions work.
By 1918, 1 million women across
the nation were employed in this
hazardous work, handling explosives
such as TNT, and in munitions
factories women also served as police
officers, checking that dangerous
substances were not being brought
into the establishments. The dangers
posed were clearly illustrated on 19

January 1917, when an explosion at
a munitions factory in Silvertown,
East London killed 73 people and
injured 400. Besides those employed
in industrial jobs, 100,000 women
joined the Women's Auxiliary Army
Corps (WAAC), the Women's Royal
Naval Service (Wrens), and the
Women's Royal Air Force (WRAF).

An unexpected result of World
War I was the emergence of women's
football teams to represent the
munitions factories, one of the
most successful being the one that
represented the huge AEC munitions
factory at Beckton in East London.
These female teams competed in their
own league and used league grounds
until this was prohibited in 1921. A
further unexpected – and to some
observers unwelcome – development
was the practice of women wearing
trousers. These proved to be more
convenient garments to wear in many
industrial jobs than skirts, so of course
the idea caught on. This development
naturally attracted the disapproval of
some until the Bright Young Things
of the 1920s also started to adopt
trousers, as they began to dominate
the post-war social scene in London.

THE VOTE

But the most lasting consequence of World War I was enacted in legislation during its closing months. The contribution of women to the war effort effectively demolished the arguments of those who had opposed the suffragettes in their campaign for the vote. In February 1918, the Representation of the People Act gave the vote to all women over 30 and all men over 21. The younger women had to wait another ten years for the vote, but they didn't have to wait so long for the first woman to enter Parliament: Nancy Astor took her seat in 1919.

WORLD WAR II

Standing in line
Queuing becomes a pastime

In January 1940, bacon, butter and sugar were rationed, and rationing of further food categories was introduced during the months that followed. Although bread and vegetables were not rationed during World War II itself, as the result of a poor wheat harvest, bread was rationed from the middle of 1946 to 1948. During the war a number of foods upon which the diets of the poor depended, including bread itself, flour, potatoes, oatmeal and eggs, were actually subsidized by the government.

The existence of rationing did not, of course, eliminate the need for queuing. Indeed queuing became a national pastime for Londoners and the rest of Britain during this time, with people occasionally joining queues without knowing what they were queuing for – just with the hope that at the head of the queue there would be some rare and usually unavailable substance. Indeed, it was reported that one housewife arrived home in a state of high excitement because she had managed to buy some boiled sweets and a tin of evaporated milk.

The rationing of clothes caused particular anguish. In London, an assistant working in a Bond Street store wrote to the novelist George Orwell that her customers were already so well supplied with clothes that rationing didn't affect them as much as it did the poor who had few clothes, especially warm ones. In response, Orwell argued that clothes rationing should continue after the war until everyone was equally shabby!

healthy British bread for the same reason. In the years following the war, the British public has gradually come to regard wholemeal bread as more wholesome and tasty than their ancestors did.

HOORAY FOR THE KAISER AND HITLER!

It had long been understood that wholemeal bread, which contains a higher proportion of fibres or roughage, was more nutritious than white bread. Nevertheless, the British population regarded white bread, from which most of the fibre had been removed, as more desirable.

However during World War I, the Kaiser unexpectedly came to the rescue of the wholemeal loaf. U-boats threatened the Atlantic convoys, so the resulting shortage of wheat obliged millers to extract more from their limited supplies, thus leaving more of the beneficial fibres within the flour.

At the end of World War I, the British population resumed its customary preference for white bread. However, in World War II Hitler became the unlikely saviour of

London to the Lake District
Pioneers in search for a healthy diet

As well as between warriors, World War II was also fought between scientists. And not all of these scientists were designing weapons like radar, or cracking the codes of the German Enigma machine at Bletchley Park. Some were ensuring that the population was adequately fed for the ordeals it faced, and the British won this particular war hands down. Before World War II the country had imported about half the food it consumed, importing a much larger proportion of products like sugar, fruit, cereals and fats. But during the war, the process of importing food across the Atlantic entailed a perilous sea voyage, beset by German U-boats.

During the 1930s, a school medical officer had devised the improbably named Glossop sandwich for under-nourished schoolchildren in Derbyshire's High Peak; during World War II its use was extended to cities like London. In fact, this sandwich was a menu of milk, fruit, wholemeal bread, margarine enriched by vitamins, oily fish like sardines, cheese, watercress and yeast. It proved surprisingly popular as well as nutritious, pointing to a healthier future.

Thus in January 1940, a particularly cold month when bacon, butter and sugar started to be rationed, a group of scientists set out from Cambridge for the Lake District. Many of them cycled to settle in a spartan cottage named Robin Ghyll in Langdale, a particularly remote part of the beautiful but unforgiving landscape between Kendal and Kirkby Stephen. This cottage belonged to the famous Cambridge historian G M Trevelyan, and for the next nine days the scientists subjected themselves to a ruthless programme of diet and physical exercise.

A 6am start was followed by walking 36 miles a day on foot. Scafell Pike was scaled, followed by the terrifying Wrynose and Hardknott passes and other Lake District heights. If you doubt their fortitude, take a look at a map! To make things a little tougher, and to replicate the hard physical work that many war workers would have to undertake, the scientists carried rucksacks filled with bricks and similarly unyielding objects weighing between 15kg and 20kg (34lbs and 44lbs). Try walking to the shops with that! The nutritional content of their food was carefully measured each day, including the

Enigma machine

calorific value, as was their weight and other aspects of their wellbeing.

The group then returned to London, where they, with others, devised a diet that would make the optimum use of available food, thereby ensuring that the need for imported foodstuffs during the war was kept to a minimum. One of their simpler measures was the addition of calcium carbonate (chalk to you and me) to wholemeal bread to make up for the shortage of calcium caused by the rationing of some dairy products – this practice has continued ever since. Their diet was far more vegetarian than the one beforehand – for example, they identified that it was more efficient to grow a field of cereal and feed it to the population than it was to feed the cereal to animals and use their meat as food. The diet was also healthier, containing more protein and carbohydrate and less fat than previously.

As a result of these scientists' efforts, the British population as a whole was better fed during the war than at any time before – or in many cases since. Productivity of factories in areas of poverty increased many times over, as the previously malnourished population began to thrive. In London, this was notable in the poor areas to the east and south-east of the city where the factories that produced war materials were located. The only adverse consequence reported of the diet was a marked increase in flatulence – not good in the confined space of a London air raid shelter! Two of the scientists were Robert McCance and Elsie Widdowson, and their pioneering work in measuring the nutritional qualities of foods is still regularly updated and republished to enable dieticians to carry on their work – McCance and Widdowson are to food what Wisden is to cricket.

GRANDSON OF DARWIN'S BULLDOG

One of the scientists who pioneered a healthier diet during World War II was the 22-year-old Andrew Huxley (1917–2012), who was the half-brother of the British writer Aldous Huxley. Andrew was also the

*grandson of Thomas Henry Huxley,
who was known as Darwin's Bulldog.
This was because in 1859 Thomas
had fiercely defended Darwin's* **On
the Origin of Species** *against
foolish criticism from 'Soapy Sam'
Wilberforce, then the Bishop
of Oxford.*

*Andrew Huxley, Thomas's last
surviving grandson, went on to
make his own contribution to
science, working for the Admiralty
and the RAF during World War II
then winning the Nobel Prize for
Physiology or Medicine in 1963. In
fact, it is the late Sir Andrew Huxley
to whom your author is indebted for
this account of the development of the
wartime diet.*

What did they live on?
Weekly allowances in 1945

On what did Londoners subsist during World War II? Here are some examples of weekly allowances per person in April 1945, as the war in Europe was drawing to a close:

Bacon and ham: 113g (4oz)
Sugar: 227g (8oz)
Tea: 57g (2oz)
Meat: to the value of 6p
(around £2 at today's value)
Cheese: 85g (3oz)
Jam or marmalade: 113g (4oz)
Butter: 57g (2oz)
Margarine: 113g (4oz)
Lard (fat): 57g (2oz)
Sweets: 85g (3oz)

Try measuring out those amounts and living on them! You might manage a day or so, but not much longer. However citizens with special

Ration book

needs, such as pregnant women and those in physically demanding occupations, received more generous allowances than those shown. Also bread, fruit and vegetables, including potatoes, were not rationed, although sometimes they were in short supply.

The whole system was administered through ration books: one was issued to each citizen, with mothers being responsible for their children's. Each book contained a number of weekly coupons for each of the commodities listed, and for many others besides. People living in London and other British cities had fewer opportunities to supplement their diets than country dwellers, where deals could be done with farmers in exchange for unwanted cigarette or petrol coupons.

Petrol too was much in demand, despite the price being increased to 1 shilling and 9 pence a gallon – this is the equivalent to about 45p a litre at today's value!

Ivor Novello

FALLEN IDOL

One of the most newsworthy events of World War II concerned the imprisonment of London's leading matinee idol, Ivor Novello (1893–1951). One of the best-known actors, composers and dramatists of his generation, he composed 'Keep the Home Fires Burning', one of the most popular songs of World War I. Then in 1939, following a series of successes, he produced The Dancing Years, the most popular show of the war in which Novello himself took the lead role.

In 1944 he was given some petrol coupons for his Rolls Royce by an admirer who had stolen them from her employer – as an accessory, Novello was therefore sentenced to a short term in prison. Noel Coward, his fellow dramatist, suggested that Novello had done nothing special for the war effort, yet when he returned to the stage in **The Dancing Years** *his first entrance was greeted with enthusiastic applause.*

Spivs at your service
Nylons, whisky, knicker elastic – you name it, guv!

During World War II, a black market flourished in London and across the rest of Britain operated by people known as spivs. These were the kind represented by the fictional character of Private Joe Walker from the BBC's *Dad's Army*, who could always 'lay his hands' on extra supplies of rationed items in exchange for cash. The activities of the so-called spivs lasted as long as rationing, which did not end until 4 July 1954 when, amidst general rejoicing, meat was

finally removed from the ration.

In the meantime, ex-Private Joe Walker, or someone just like him, would appear unexpectedly on a London street, wearing a loud suit and driving a van, the latter loaded with items such as jars of jam, bottles of whisky, butter, eggs or, most precious of all, nylon stockings. The contents of the van would rapidly vanish, as would then the van itself and its driver, before the authorities arrived on the scene.

IN HEAVY DEMAND
One essential item of feminine attire was virtually always in short supply during World War II: namely, the silk stocking. Nylon had been invented in the USA in 1930 and used to make stockings from 1938, but during the war both nylon and silk were in heavy demand for parachutes. This meant that any German, or indeed RAF, pilot who bailed out was likely to see his parachute disappear for conversion into black market stockings.

However, even with such ingenuity the demand for the material greatly

Nylon stockings or pencil lines?

exceeded the supply. In the absence of such comforts, many London women resorted to dying their legs nylon brown with gravy browning to create the impression they were wearing stockings even though they weren't. And in the days when stockings had seams, these would be replicated by a pencil line drawn at the rear of the calf and thigh.

Man of vision
Lord Woolton at the Ministry of Food

U pon the outbreak of World War II, Frederick Marquis, 1st Earl of Woolton (1883–1964), was appointed by Prime Minister Neville Chamberlain to head a Ministry of Food. He had been a successful executive in Lewis's department store in Liverpool, where he was also active in social work. Despite this unusual background Lord Woolton was to prove an inspired choice – however, he did not get off to the most promising start.

First he proposed the Basal Diet, which included fat, but no meat or fish at all. By this time Winston Churchill had been appointed Prime Minister and informed Woolton: 'The way to lose the war is to try to force the British Public into a diet of milk, oatmeal, potatoes etc. washed down on gala occasions with a little lime juice'. A further proposal to encourage the British public to eat their pets was also quietly dropped!

As he settled into his new role, Lord Woolton proceeded to engage the services of a number of leading figures, some of whom were to become celebrities in their different fields. One of these, Magnus Pyke, later became a well-known television personality, noted for his waving arms and strong advocacy of the benefits of purple-sprouting broccoli, for a long time an almost unknown although highly nutritious vegetable.

Marguerite Patten OBE was one of the best known among the eminent chefs and writers recruited to devise recipes that made imaginative use of available ingredients. Her *Victory Cookbook* contained unfamiliar but nourishing recipes such as parsnip and sage soup, smoked haddock and leek kedgeree, and venison hot pot.

By such means, a daily intake of 2,500 kilocalories for men and 2,000 kilocalories for women was both recommended and achieved. By contrast, in agriculturally rich France, where the German occupiers appropriated much of the produce, the daily intake barely exceeded 1,800 kilocalories – in more deprived areas it struggled to reach half that level, leading to severe malnutrition.

The best known of British wartime foods was named after the minister: Woolton Pie was a vegetable pie devised in the kitchens of the Savoy hotel of London. It consisted of potatoes, swedes, parsnips, carrots, onions, cauliflower, turnips and oats, topped with pastry made from potatoes then sprinkled with grated cheese. We are now encouraged to eat a healthy diet of five fruit and vegetable portions a day, yet Woolton Pie exceeded that on its own!

The wartime Ministry of Food also promoted much-derided rhymes to minimize the waste of food:

Those who have the will to win
Eat potatoes in their skin,
Knowing that the sight of peelings
Deeply hurts Lord Woolton's feelings.

And even the skins that were thrown away did not go to waste. In London's Tottenham area, a salvage depot segregated all food waste and devised a method for making use of food waste from homes, hotels, schools and restaurants. The waste was heated and turned into a firm,

Queen Mary

pudding-like texture that became known as Tottenham Pudding – this was widely adopted for feeding pigs and poultry. A 1940 photograph showed Queen Mary, Elizabeth II's grandmother, inspecting what looks like a bath full of this unappetizing substance at the Tottenham salvage depot. She shows no inclination to sample it, but the pigs and poultry loved it – in due course, they were themselves turned into bacon, ham and chicken.

FORGET THE SNOEK

One of Lord Woolton's undoubted failures was snoek. Fish and chips were not rationed during the war, which helped to confirm this dish as central to the London and British diet. They were easily portable in yesterday's newspapers, making fish and chips Britain's first takeaway food; moreover, the seas around Britain contained abundant supplies of fish. The popularity of this abundant food source meant that trawlermen were exempt from military service, although they sometimes fell victim to German attacks.

So when attempts were made to supplement the traditional British cod, plaice, sole and haddock with plentiful supplies of a fish named snoek (pronounced 'snook') from South Africa, the taste buds across the capital rebelled. After all, in 1860 a Jewish fishmonger from the East End of London named Joseph Malin first introduced fish and chips to the nation, so Londoners were connoisseurs in the matter! Snoek was thought to be lacking in taste, and any taste it did possess was not *for British palates – it was therefore mostly fed to cats. People preferred to queue, as they often had to, since fish was not always readily available.*

Nowhere is sacred
London digs for victory

One of the best-known posters used during World War II was known as 'Dig for Victory', which encouraged people to transform land into allotments to grow vegetables and raise livestock. But the forbears of Richard Briers and Felicity Kendal in the BBC comedy *The Good Life* were not choosing a lifestyle – they were growing food to survive. Thus London householders fortunate enough to have gardens were quick to turn over their flowerbeds and lawns to the cultivation of fruits and vegetables; those less fortunate colonized bombsites for the duration of the war. By the end of World War II, it is estimated that there were 30,000 allotments in London, of which about 6,000 were in London's parks.

Nowhere was sacred. The Rugby Football Union's ground at Twickenham was turned over to allotments, which was not an inappropriate use given that the stadium was built on land previously known as Billy Williams' Cabbage Patch and is still referred to as the Cabbage Patch by many in the know. Meanwhile, the grass of Wimbledon's sacred courts was devoted to growing vegetables and grazing sheep. The squares of Bloomsbury were devoted to allotments – this was despite reservations expressed by their owner, the Duke of Bedford. The Ministry of Food opened a demonstration allotment on Park Lane in Mayfair, although its value was compromised when its lettuces and shallots were stolen one night in 1942. In the window boxes of Chatham House in St James's Square, tomatoes replaced geraniums.

On the roof of New Zealand House, the High Commissioner kept beehives to supply honey; nearby, the caretaker's son grew wheat to feed his father's chickens. Not to be outdone, on the roof of 55 Broadway, the headquarters of London Transport, the Chief Engineer grew beans, marrows and tomatoes. The wife of the Keeper of Coins and Medals grew peas, beans, onions and lettuces in the forecourt of the British Museum. Pig clubs were popular among air raid wardens and police officers, who raised their own porkers. Even the Ladies' Carlton Club in Pall Mall, not to be confused with the male bastion of the same name, turned over its swimming pool to pig rearing.

In August 1942, the Ministry of Food organized an Off the Ration Exhibition to encourage the rearing of animals for food, which was rather ominously staged at London Zoo. The elephants and other residents of this establishment were safe, but a photograph taken at the exhibition shows a group of children, under the gaze of the Duke of Norfolk who opened the event, fondly handling a small white rabbit. One fears for the future of the animal!

Not fine dining
*Eating out in London
during the war*

London restaurants remained open during World War II, although their menus were limited: they were only permitted to serve three courses plus beverages, the price being limited to 5 shillings per head (around £5 at today's value). This situation did not satisfy everyone; indeed, there were reports of diners storming out of smart London restaurants complaining that the portions of cream were inadequate.

Among the most popular restaurants at the time were those run by Lyons, notably their Corner Houses on the Strand, Coventry Street and Oxford Street. Each of these had a brasserie, a grillroom, and later

Home-grown produce

an egg and bacon room that was popular with students. The Oxford Street Corner House remained open throughout the Blitz, apart from just three days in September 1940 during the Battle of Britain when it had no water supply. A menu has survived from the wartime days of this establishment: customers were offered a three course meal for 1 shilling and 6 pence (around £1.50 at today's value) with a choice of two starters, seven main courses, three desserts, and a small cup of coffee.

Meanwhile, early in the war the Ministry of Food announced that Community Feeding Centres, run by the local authorities, would provide simple nourishing meals at low prices. In Kilburn, the formidable Flora Solomon started one of the first of these. Born Flora Benenson in Tsarist Russia, she berated Simon Marks, her fellow Jew and son of the founder of Marks & Spencer, for the fact that his staff could not afford to eat in the firm's staff canteens. Marks subsequently hired her as the company's welfare officer, and when the war began she applied her energy and skill to feeding the population

of Kilburn from its Community Feeding Centre.

When Churchill became Prime Minister in 1940, he changed the rather grim name of the Community Feeding Centres to British Restaurants, and these flourished from 1940 to the end of the war. Some of them were run by the Salvation Army, some by Quakers, and many by local authorities. By 1943, approximately 2,160 British Restaurants – 200 of them in London – were serving 600,000 meals a day. Smaller towns that could not support their own restaurants had what were called Cash and Carries instead. Here, the meals were prepared at the larger British Restaurants and then delivered to these smaller units, ready to eat.

Primarily in London but also across the rest of Britain, mobile canteens in vans that could visit shelters and serve heated food supplemented both the Community Feeding Centres and the Cash and Carries. On 14 November 1940, Coventry was devastated by an air raid, leaving much of the city without power or water. Therefore, the following day 40 mobile canteens were despatched from London to Coventry to feed the victims.

The meals in a British Restaurant during the war cost around 9 pence each (a little less than £1 at today's value), although this could be cheaper in some areas. They would typically consist of two or three courses – a main course and a dessert, plus a cup of tea, sometimes also with soup as a starter – and were often prepared in schools, whose kitchens were well suited to this kind of mass food preparation.

No British Restaurant main course could have more than one portion of meat, fish, poultry, game, cheese or eggs. Among the foods on offer was the Woolton Sandwich (see Man of Vision), which consisted of ground raw vegetables laced with chutney. More popular was the Blitz Broth, similar to medieval peasant food and made with seasonal vegetables, pulses, cereals, and when available, meat. This was both thick and nutritious, and had been devised by Lord Woolton's adviser, the nutritionist Jack Drummond (see Family Tragedy).

Factory workers often used British Restaurants during their lunch

breaks, one of the busiest and most successful being located in Woolmore Street, in the much-bombed area of Poplar in East London. In particular, the restaurant was much used by women engaged in wartime work in a nearby engineering works. The public's view of the restaurants varied from the enthusiastic to the disdainful. However, the fact that they were so much used suggests that the food was as good as any available elsewhere at reasonable cost.

Indeed, the Town Clerk of Acton reacted vigorously when it was suggested by an official from the Ministry of Food that the food served in the British Restaurant in Standard Road, Acton, was of poor quality, observing that 800 factory workers used it every day. The official hastily insisted that he had been misunderstood. Moreover, when there was talk of closing the chain of British Restaurants in May 1945, following the celebration of Victory in Europe, there was widespread dismay across the capital. In spite of this, they were closed soon after the General Election of the same year.

FAMILY TRAGEDY

The menus for the British Restaurants were devised with the help of Jack Drummond (1891–1952). Before World War II, Drummond and others had made extensive studies of the British diet, exposing its many inadequacies. Tragically, in August 1952 Drummond, together with his wife Anne and ten-year-old daughter Elizabeth, was brutally murdered in France.

The family was camping by the side of the N96, near the hamlet of La Brillane in the valley of the Durance in the department of Alpes-de-Haute-Provence. Drummond and his wife were shot, and their daughter was battered to death with the stock of a carbine. Gaston Dominici, the peasant farmer on whose land the family was camping, was jailed for the murder but later released by President Charles de Gaulle.

A memorial to the family, who are buried in Forcalquier, can be found close to the site of their murder.

Covering costs
Women's Voluntary Service to the rescue

British Restaurants (see Not Fine Dining) aimed to cover their costs and most did, a small number even making a modest profit for their local authorities. One of the reasons their meals were so cheap was that these restaurants were often run with the help of unpaid volunteers from the Women's Voluntary Service (WVS) – which, rather belatedly in 1966, became the Women's *Royal* Voluntary Service.

Clad in their distinctive green uniforms – for which they had to pay, using their precious clothes coupons – the WVS swiftly arrived on the scene following a bombing raid or another disaster, dispensing tea from a mobile canteen, sympathy, and sometimes first aid. Yet their less evident but crucial work was often done behind the scenes, notably at the 200 British Restaurants of wartime London.

One of the other services provided by the WVS was that of the Rinso Mobile Emergency Units that operated in the capital. Each unit, equipped with its own van, would visit blitzed areas, mostly in East and South London, to collect clothing and linen from people who had lost their homes and had no means of doing their own laundry. They would take the laundry to a depot with its own power and water supply then return it to their owners freshly laundered.

WVS mobile canteen

GERMAN MODEL

The Women's Voluntary Service (WVS) was founded in 1938, as war approached and it became evident that such an organization was likely to be needed. In the same year Frank Pick, Vice Chairman of the London Passenger Transport Board (later London Transport), was approached by the government and asked to help promote the new organization and encourage recruitment.

Pick was chosen because of his pioneering work in art, design and advertising for London's network of buses and trains. He thus asked two of his young assistants to find a suitable photograph of a young woman to pose as a WVS volunteer on posters, telling them that she should be 'good looking and courageous' rather than too glamorous.

Following a search through a number of picture agencies, a suitable image was found and widely used – with great success. Many women joined the WVS, their numbers eventually reaching 850,000. Intrigued by the identity of the young model, press enquiries were made

concerning her identity – she turned
out to be German. This embarrassing
fact remained a secret until one of the
team who found the model revealed it
to your author, 60 years later.

Miracles of science
Spirit of ingenuity among
wartime advertisers

Advertisers of some rather
unlikely products were not
slow to exploit the shortage of food
across London and the rest of Britain
during World War II to promote their
own merchandise. This advertising
sometimes took the form of cartoons,
which depicted a housewife's
dilemma as she struggled to feed her
family on a limited budget, further
constrained by rationing and the
accompanying coupons.

One typical example of such
a cartoon was supposedly based
upon the experience of a London
housewife, whose mother overhears
her neighbours discussing the sickly
state of her daughter's children,
which they attribute to inadequate
nourishment. Father, brandishing his

Bile beans advertisement

pipe, is unsympathetic, but he agrees
to consult 'Old Jock' about it at work
the next day. (Was the name of Old
Jock chosen for the advertisement
because it implied a canny and thrifty
Scotsman?)

In any case, Old Jock comes
up trumps and recommends 'pre-
digested cocoa' from a well-known
manufacturer – still flourishing,
but no longer making cocoa – and
the result is miraculous. Having
consumed this unsavoury sounding

substance, the mother's three children pronounce that they are full up after all their meals – although presumably consuming the same diet as before apart from the cocoa. How this miracle of nutritional science is achieved is far from clear, although the rules for advertising were far slacker in those days.

Naturally, other products jumped on the nutritional bandwagon. Mackintosh's Quality Street, readers were told, 'is a food', adding the reassuring 'although you don't have to fry it'. It was, the advertisement insisted, 'scientifically determined' that the Quality Street assortment, weight for weight, was richer in calories than steak, eggs or bread.

Other advertisements featured bile beans for women to tone up the system, purify the blood and remove residues – they were a laxative, supposedly based on a recipe from Australian Aborigines. Meanwhile, Wills Goldflake cigarettes were aimed at men, especially troops, to give them the 'Wills to win'. One must admire the spirit of optimism and ingenuity of the wartime advertisers.

Unduly pessimistic
Bombing casualties predicted to be far worse

Prior to World War II in 1932, the Conservative politician Stanley Baldwin, in an ominous and fortunately unduly pessimistic speech in Parliament, gloomily predicted that 'the bomber will always get through'. He thereby implied that British air defences would be inadequate against determined and accurate bombing, as a result of which London and other cities would be reduced to rubble and their inhabitants to corpses.

His predictions were prompted by the fate of the Basque city of Guernica in Spain, which had no defences against the Fascist bombers of 1930. They were also based on the estimates of the Committee of Imperial Defence, which predicted that in an air raid 700 tons of bombs would produce 35,000 casualties, including 10,000 dead. Films with similarly apocalyptic representations of air raids had further stimulated such fears. In the face of such prospects the government decreed that the London Underground

Railway would be needed to evacuate the corpses. As in World War I, the London Underground's use as shelter from air raids was therefore restricted – but as we shall see later, Londoners decided otherwise (see Shelter from Hitler's Wrath).

However the casualty estimates, using sophisticated mathematical calculations based on the effects of shelling in World War I, failed to take into account the fact that many bombers did not 'get through' in the face of anti-aircraft measures. Also that the accuracy of their bombing from great heights was such that most devices fell far from their intended targets. As such, although London was bombed for 57 consecutive nights in the Blitz from 7 September 1940, the total deaths in the city amounted to about 20,000 – the expected tally for just two heavy raids.

Now celebrated as Battle of Britain Day, the battle in the skies over Britain on 15 September 1940 became a decisive event in World War II. So great were the German losses on that day, and so great was the weight of opposition their airmen met from Fighter

Surviving the London Blitz

Command's Spitfires and Hurricanes that they, and their Reichsmarschall Goering, realized that the battle was lost and that their dreams of invading Britain were at an end. At the end of the battle the RAF had more fighters than they had at the start, whereas the Luftwaffe had lost more than half of their bombers and almost 1,000 fighter planes, along with their crews.

Thereafter the Luftwaffe continued to bomb London until May 1941,

when they turned their attentions east to Russia. They bombed at night when they were less vulnerable to the RAF, and it was this night bombing that became known by the press and subsequently Londoners as the Blitz. The word 'Blitz' is derived from the German word *Blitzkrieg*, which actually means 'lightning'. Yet the only lights involved in the Blitz were the searchlights of the British anti-aircraft defences.

HULL FIRE CORNER

Accounts of the Blitz have tended to focus on London, which suffered more bombing than any other single city, yet many other British cities were severely bombed. The most notorious of these attacks was the one on Coventry, but ports like Liverpool were also subjected to frequent air raids. Although a much smaller community, the port of Hull on the Humber estuary can claim to have suffered proportionally more damage than London between June 1940 and March 1945. Over that period 1,000 hours of air raid alerts occurred in the city, with

some 5,000 homes destroyed and 95 per cent of domestic dwellings damaged. This led to the deaths of 1,200 people, while 3,000 were injured and 152,000 made homeless – almost half the city's population of 320,000. So the Blitz wasn't all about London.

Shelter from Hitler's wrath
London decides how the Tube is to be used

Following the guidance of the Committee of Imperial Defence and its gloomy prognostications that 10,000 deaths would result from each air raid in the forthcoming apocalypse (see Unduly Pessimistic), posters were placed in London's Underground stations. They read: 'The public are informed that, in order to operate the railways for essential movement, Underground stations cannot be used as air raid shelters. In any event a number of stations would have to be cleared for safety in certain contingencies'. In the early months of World War II, prior to the London

Blitz, no one felt the need to shelter in the Underground.

However, on the evening of 24 August 1940 this situation changed. Hitler had initially forbidden the bombing of London, instead preferring to concentrate on destroying the RAF in the Battle of Britain, as preparation for invasion. Yet on that fateful evening, a German pilot who had failed to find his target was returning to his base in France with his bombs still onboard, a landing hazard. Thus, when his navigator informed him that the plane was over open country, these bombs were duly jettisoned. However, they fell on what is now the Barbican in the heart of the City of London, where they struck the historic medieval church of St Giles–without–Cripplegate. Needless to say, Hitler was not pleased.

The pilot was duly reprimanded, but Hitler was further enraged when Churchill ordered an immediate retaliatory raid on Berlin. This inflicted little damage, but Goering had previously publicly promised that no bomb would ever fall on the German capital. Further

embarrassment was caused when Hitler repaired to a shelter with the Russian Foreign Minister, Molotov: he had been trying to assure the Russian that the British were finished and the war was over. 'In that case,' said Molotov, 'whose bombs are those falling and why are we in this shelter?'

Hitler immediately ordered Goering to redirect his bombers from their previous RAF airfield targets to London and other British cities. Thus between 7 September and 13 November 1940 London was bombed every night, apart from 2 November when bad weather intervened. The result of this was that London and Britain's other cities were devastated, yet the British airfields were saved and the Battle of Britain was won within three weeks.

In the meantime, the population of London had to find somewhere to shelter during the onslaught of the Blitz. On 8 September 1940, a crowd seeking shelter forced their way past helpless officials, police and soldiers to occupy the platforms of Liverpool Street Underground station. In the words of *Picture Post*: 'London decided how the tube stations were to be used'.

ST GILES-WITHOUT-CRIPPLEGATE

St Giles's Church in the heart of the Barbican complex in London survived the Luftwaffe, and after

St Giles-without-Cripplegate

the war the building was fully and sympathetically restored. Today it remains a charming medieval church in the midst of the towers and glass of Cripplegate. The church lies close to the area where Shakespeare lived during his early years in London; he would surely have worshipped there, as did John Bunyan and Daniel Defoe. Oliver Cromwell was married at St Giles in 1620, and the church contains the graves of the poet John Milton, and the Elizabethan sailor Martin Frobisher. John Foxe, author of **Foxe's Book of Martyrs,** *was also buried there.*

Spitfires from saucepans?
Lord Beaverbrook embraces the war effort

One of the figures that came to national prominence during World War II was Max Aitken, 1st Baron Beaverbrook (1879–1964). Born in Canada, as a young man he made a fortune in cement and newspapers then moved to England in 1910. Here he became friendly with fellow Canadian Andrew Bonar Law, who was briefly Prime Minister after World War I – by that time Aitken had become Baron Beaverbrook.

In 1911 Beaverbrook invested in the *Daily Express*, which he gradually built into one of the world's most successful newspapers. It also became the source of his great wealth and public reputation – although it was often a source of irritation to his Conservative friends. The *Express* occupied a specially built art deco building at 120 Fleet Street in London, and Evelyn Waugh ruthlessly caricatured the newspaper and its proprietor as

the *Daily Beast* and Lord Copper respectively in his comic novel, *Scoop*.

During the 1930s Beaverbrook was an arch-appeaser. As late as November 1939 he told the Russian Ambassador, Ivan Maisky: 'What concerns me is the fate of the British Empire… I don't understand why we must wage a three-year war to crush Hitlerism… Poland? Czechoslovakia? What are they to do with us? Cursed be the day when Chamberlain gave our guarantee to Poland'.

Despite these sentiments, Beaverbrook became close to Winston Churchill. Recognizing

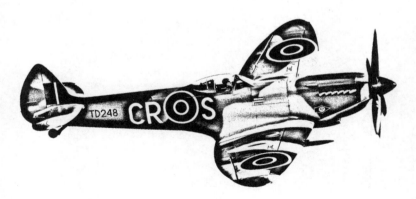

Spitfire

his energy, in 1940 Churchill made Beaverbrook Minister of Aircraft Production during the Battle of Britain. In this role the new minister tore up existing plans and produced aircraft as he had previously produced newspapers, urging citizens to donate their saucepans and garden railings to make into Spitfires and Hurricanes. Thus kitchens were emptied of their implements, and parks and gardens denuded of their railings. Very little of this metal found its way into aircraft, but people felt that they were contributing to the struggle against Hitler.

Against the odds
*Sir Keith Park defends
the airfields*

K eith Park (1892–1975) was born in New Zealand, fought at the Battle of Gallipoli in World War I, then joined the British Royal Flying Corps in 1916 where he commanded a squadron. After the war in 1919, he was appointed to the position of a flight lieutenant in the renamed Royal Air Force (RAF). Later in 1938, now promoted to the rank of air vice

marshal, Park was appointed by Sir Hugh Dowding, the head of RAF Fighter Command, to command its crucial Number 11 Group.

With responsibility for defending London and the South East of England during the Battle of Britain, Park's astute harbouring of forces in the face of the Luftwaffe's onslaught, as well as his morale boosting trips to his airfields in his personal Hurricane fighter, secured British success in the battle. This was despite the disputes that took place between him and his colleague Trafford Leigh-Mallory, who was in charge of Number 12 Group and responsible for the defence of the Midlands and East Anglia.

During the Battle of Britain, Leigh-Mallory was asked to devote his squadrons to defending Park's airfields. However, supported by his most famous and contentious pilot, the legless ace Douglas Bader, he instead became obsessed with employing the Big Wing tactic, which involved large numbers of aircraft flying to oppose the German forces in wing-sized formation. Thus, by the time Leigh-Mallory's aircraft arrived to defend Park's airfields, much damage had already been done.

Despite these difficulties, Park was recognized as the commander whose hour-by-hour deployments of limited resources had ensured the Luftwaffe did not succeed in its plan to destroy the RAF as an effective force. The fighter ace and later Air Vice Marshal Johnnie Johnson said of Park, 'He was the only man who could have lost the war in a day or even an afternoon' – even Douglas Bader made a similar acknowledgement of Park's crucial role. After World War II, Park retired to his native New Zealand.

Hugh Dowding

'STUFFY' DOWDING

Hugh Dowding (1882–1970), later Baron Dowding, was one of the great commanders of World War II. He joined the Royal Artillery as a young man, transferring to the Royal Flying Corps as a pilot during World War I, and was then appointed to head the new Fighter Command in 1936. Dowding was one of very few who did not believe Stanley Baldwin's 1932 assertion that 'the bomber will always get through' (see Unduly Pessimistic).

Prior to World War II, Dowding therefore set about proving his point by commissioning new and far more powerful fighter aircraft, such as the Spitfire and Hurricane. He also established the network of Chain Home radar installations to provide Britain with an early warning of attacks. Defying Churchill's attempts to send precious squadrons to defend France when her forces were collapsing, he thereby ensured that when the Luftwaffe's onslaught began on Britain, the RAF was ready for it.

Dowding enjoyed the confidence

*of his pilots, who nicknamed him
'Stuffy' owing to his dour personality
and lack of humour. He retired from
his post after the Battle of Britain in
1940, devoting the rest of his life to
campaigning for the humane treatment
of animals. His ashes were buried
beneath the Battle of Britain Memorial
Window in Westminster Abbey, and
his statue stands opposite that of Sir
Arthur Harris outside the church of St
Clement Dane's, also in Westminster.*

Making the best of it
*Subterranean communities
in the Tube*

As the Blitz on London began, the British government set about organizing London Underground stations as shelters, making them safe and comfortable. A census at the end of September 1940 revealed that 177,000 people were using London shelters, about half of the numbers found using them during World War I when bombing was minimal. The Labour MP and Home Secretary, Herbert Morrison, introduced shelter wardens and lavatories, as well as a ticketing system so people did not have to queue all day to be admitted when they should have been at work.

Seventy-nine Underground stations were eventually designated as shelters in London, together with disused and partly completed tunnels such as the short Piccadilly Line branch from Holborn to Aldwych that was closed for the duration of the war. Aldwych station, eventually closed permanently in 1994, was later used as a film set, notably for one of the closing scenes in the film *The Battle of Britain*. Season tickets were issued to regular shelter users for specific platform spaces, a measure designed to frustrate the spivs who were queuing and selling on the tickets. J Lyons and Co. ran Tube Refreshment Specials during the night, delivering tea, cocoa and milk, and collecting the previous night's empties. In many shelters, three-tier bunk beds were installed along the platform walls, together accommodating 22,000 people.

However, not all visitors were welcome. In the early days of the Blitz, the Germans concentrated their attacks on the commercial heart of the capital and the East End in an attempt to destroy the docks. Some people from the West End decided to pay visits to their less fortunate compatriots who were sheltering in the Tube. However, their patronising behaviour was not appreciated, at least one such party being roughly handled and sent packing.

Soon the shelters on the London Underground became a separate, subterranean community with clubs formed for chess, dominoes and darts – indeed, an inter-shelter darts league soon flourished. Dressmaking classes were particularly popular, since they showed pupils how to make best use

Sheltering on the London Underground

of the scarce materials available. The Council for the Encouragement of Music and the Arts (the forerunner of the post-war Arts Council) sent performers and recordings of classical music into the shelters, although on one occasion the unappreciative occupants complained that the music was drowning the sound of the bombing!

Films were also shown, and an amateur theatrical company visited many shelters with a production of some of Chekhov's plays. Less elevated entertainment was provided by ENSA (the Entertainments National Service Association), less flatteringly described by one performer as 'Every Night Something Awful'. Nevertheless, on one occasion such a performance featured the celebrated George Formby, perilously suspended above the tracks with his ukulele – presumably someone had switched off the current.

South Kensington station was one of many that set up small hospitals to deal with the sick, or in a few cases, mothers in labour – indeed, children were born in this subterranean world. Thirty-six doctors and 200 nurses served these medical units in London, and treatment was free – a foretaste of the National Health Service that was to follow when the war ended. There was a plague of head lice and mosquito bites among shelterers, the insects attracted by the warmth of the tunnels. Moreover, in 1998 two scientists from Queen Mary and Westfield College identified a new species of mosquito that had evolved in the tunnels.

At Christmas 1940, at the height of the Blitz, raffles were organized to raise funds for children's Christmas parties. The Swiss Cottage underground shelter produced its own newspaper called *De Profundis*, meaning 'from the depths'. The publication's first edition was addressed to: 'Our nightly companions, our temporary cave dwellers, our sleeping companions, somnambulists, snorers, chatterers and all who inhabit the Swiss Cottage station from dusk to dawn. This is the first in a series of announcements issued in the name of co-operation, so that we may find what comfort and amenities there may be in this our nightly place of refuge'. The second edition offered 'Expert Advice', including the sage 'Vibration

due to heavy gunfire or other causes will be felt much less if you do not lie with your head against the wall'.

NOT ALL SWEETNESS AND LIGHT

At any one time about 200,000 Londoners sought protection in the Underground stations during the Blitz, but comfort and harmony were often lacking. Some people, unable to find a space on the platforms, had to sleep on escalators; others were unfortunate in their choice of sleeping space.

The following conversation was recorded in a central London tube shelter on 25 September 1940. The first speaker is an irascible elderly lady who was sleeping close to the station lavatory and whose sleep was being interrupted by the needs of other residents:

'Seventy-eight people want to go to the lavatory.'
'Can't you shut up you bleeding hypocrite?'
'I want to go to sleep and these people keep on wanting to go to the lavatory.'

It is not therefore surprising that on average men only managed four and a half hours of sleep a night, while women had to make do with three and a half. In April 1943 it was estimated that at one time or another as many as 600,000 people had made use of the tube shelters on at least one occasion.

No guarantee of safety
Death in the London Underground

Shelter in the London Underground was not an absolute guarantee of safety during the Blitz of World War II. On 12 October 1940, a bomb penetrated the surface of Whitehall and entered Trafalgar Square station on the Bakerloo Line, killing seven people. This station no longer exists, having been replaced by Charing Cross station in 1979.

On 13 October 1940, Bounds Green station on the northern extension of the Piccadilly Line was the scene of a particularly tragic incident. A homeless family of Belgian refugees, who had fled their country at the time of the Dunkirk

evacuation, had made a temporary home at the station. On that particular evening, they welcomed and made space for an English family who had been bombed out of two homes – the 16 Belgians and three English were all killed when a bomb penetrated to the station platforms. Another shelterer, an elderly lady who survived the carnage, was phlegmatic in a way that was to become characteristic of many, commenting: 'We'll sleep well tonight, at least there will be no trains coming through'.

On the following day, 14 October 1940, a bomb damaged a water main on the Northern Line at Balham, sending water and debris cascading along the station platforms where 600 were seeking shelter. This incident resulted in the death of 68 people, many of them drowned, while others were injured by debris swept along in the flood.

The most spectacular attack occurred at Bank station in the heart of the City, during the firebombing on the night of 29 to 30 December 1940 when 11 stations were struck at the same time. A bomb landed above Bank station, causing the road to collapse into the concourse. As the bomb exploded, a train entered the station and the blast blew the driver from his seat. The 'dead man's handle' brought the train to a stop, but not in time to save passengers driven into its path by the blast. In this way 56 people died – afterwards publication of photographs of the devastation was withheld for nine months for fear of damaging morale.

alarmed by the noise and holding a baby, slipped on the steps and fell. In the disorder that followed, 173 people were crushed or suffocated.

This turned out to be the worst civilian disaster of the war, now commemorated by a plaque at the station. The subsequent raid was a minor one and the casualties probably didn't need to be there at all. Again, news of the tragedy was suppressed by the government.

TRAGIC POSTSCRIPT

The London Blitz continued until May 1941, at which time Hitler turned his attentions to the east to attack Russia so the Luftwaffe became fully engaged on the Eastern Front. Yet the most tragic episode of all was yet to come.

In London on 3 March 1943, an orderly queue of about 1,500 people started to enter Bethnal Green station in response to an air raid some distance away. A newly installed ZZ anti-aircraft battery (see Amazing Devices) was fired from Victoria Park nearby, and it appears that a young mother, possibly

Troglodytic existence
Short and long-term effects of tube life

Apart from the literary efforts of the occupants of the Swiss Cottage shelter (see Making the Best of It), the refuges of the London Underground during World War II attracted the attention of some of the country's more illustrious writers. Indeed, novelist and essayist George Orwell (1903–50) commented that many of the tube shelterers were foreigners who were 'more frightened than English people during the raids'. Then the housekeeper of the diplomat Nigel Nicolson recorded a more scathing verdict on her fellow occupants after her first night in a shelter: 'Greeks they were, sir, by the look of them. I never did hold with foreigners'. Her first night in the Tube was also her last.

More characteristically, Orwell also commented on the good order that prevailed in most shelters and their 'cleanly, normal, domesticated air. Especially the young married couples, the sort of homely, cautious types that would probably be buying their houses from a building society, tucked up together under pink counterpanes.' Having lived in

George Orwell

Burma, he also compared the bombers to mosquitoes that kept returning, although one believed that they had been killed.

But like many, Orwell also worried about the longer-term effects of this troglodytic existence on people who shunned the daylight. In March 1941 he recorded in his diary: 'The Tube stations don't now stink to any extent, the new metal bunks are quite good and the people one sees there seem contented and normal, but this is just what disquiets me. What is one to think of people who go on living this sub-human life night after night, taking it all for granted and having great fun riding round and round the Inner Circle.'

By 1943, when air raids were few and far between, about 6,000 people were still living in tube shelters. Mass Observation concluded that this hard core of users found the security and companionship congenial, and therefore had no wish to be evacuated or rehoused. However, this was evidently the full extent of the problem that Orwell had feared.

MASS OBSERVATION

The social research organization Mass Observation was founded in 1937 by the anthropologist, poet and film-maker Humphrey Jennings, who later produced some of the most famous films depicting World War II. Voluntary contributors collected and sent in records of people's opinions on such matters as the abdication of King Edward VIII, the coronation of George VI, and reactions to some of the posters produced by the Ministry of Information. The government occasionally used the material collected by Mass Observation to help form policy, and the economist J M Keynes took their reports into account when proposing taxation policy. The work of Mass Observation ceased in the 1960s, as more sophisticated forms of market research took over. However their archive, now held at the University of Sussex, is an informative record of British attitudes, especially during World War II.

'Sardines in a gigantic tin'
Great British writers experience the Blitz

While travelling to London from their cottage at Rodmell in Sussex during World War II, the modernist writer Virginia Woolf and her husband Leonard shared a cup of tea with two friendly strangers in a South London air raid shelter. In his autobiography *The Journey, Not the Arrival, Matters*, Leonard then described the shelter at Russell Square, close to his home in Bloomsbury: 'dozens of men, women and children on mattresses wrapped in sheets and blankets and lying side by side all the way down the platform as if they were sardines in a gigantic tin'. Leonard admired their fortitude but did not choose to share their shelter, preferring to take his chances by remaining in his nearby flat at Mecklenburgh Square. This was eventually bombed, but fortunately during his absence.

Many other authors have recorded their experiences in London during World War II, sometimes in their fiction. The poet John Betjeman, having been turned down for the RAF on medical grounds, joined the Observer Corps, where he was taught to use a piece of plotting apparatus known as a Heath Robinson. This was designed to enable him and his colleagues to identify the height at which enemy aircraft were flying then report the information to Fighter Command, although there is no record of his having done so.

Betjeman was soon transferred to a unit that produced films to encourage activities such as growing one's own vegetables and fruits, and economizing on fuel. This brought him into contact with a young woman named Joan Hunter Dunn, who ran the canteen at the Ministry of Information in the London University Senate House in Bloomsbury. Betjeman soon developed a crush on this lady, subsequently making her the subject of one of his best-known poems, 'A Subaltern's Love Song'.

During World War II, novelist Graham Greene was a firewatcher on the roof of St Paul's Cathedral and worked for the Ministry of Information then later the secret service, also based at London University's Senate House. This formidable art deco building thus became the model for the Ministry of Fear in Greene's novel of the same name, as well as the Ministry of Truth in George Orwell's novel *1984* (see Ministry of Truth).

GOOD VALUE

A menu has survived from the era of the kind that John Betjeman would have experienced at the hands of Joan Hunter Dunn at her canteen; prices have been translated into modern decimal currency, but for an idea of present values, they need to be multiplied by about 25:

Meat, two veg, and bread:
*   10 pence (4p)*
Fish: 10 pence (4p)
Boiled pudding and custard:
*   3 pence (1.2p)*
Milk: 3 pence (1.2p)
Stewed fruit: 3 pence (1.2p)
Cakes: 2 pence (1p)
Tea (half a pint): 1 penny (0.5p)
Coffee or cocoa: penny-ha'penny (1p)

Presumably it wasn't the food that attracted the future Poet Laureate to Miss Joan Hunter Dunn, 'Furnish'd and burnish'd by Aldershot sun'.

Bottle of milk

On the Nazi death list

Noel Coward joins the Allied war effort

Noel Coward (1899–1973) was a very successful actor, singer, composer and writer, whose works included popular stage favourites such as 'Hay Fever' and 'Blithe Spirit', as well as the hit song 'Mad Dogs and Englishmen'. When World War II began, he abandoned his theatrical work and offered his services to the war effort. Yet after a spell in British Intelligence that involved much travel, Churchill decided that Coward would do more good by entertaining the troops and the battered population. This was a task Coward undertook with great success in Africa, Asia, the USA and Britain.

To that end Coward wrote a selection of patriotic and humorous songs, such as 'London Pride' and 'Don't Let's Be Beastly to the Germans, When Our Victory is Ultimately Won'. He also wrote, starred in and co-directed the film *In Which We Serve*, an account of the career of Coward's friend Lord Louis Mountbatten in the Battle of Crete. Indeed, Coward was a great favourite with the British Royal Family, to whom Mountbatten was related. King George VI was ready to give him a knighthood, but in the event Coward had to wait until 1969 to receive that accolade.

Noel Coward was on a Nazi death list for trying to persuade the Americans to enter the war. Many others were also on this list, including the writers H G Wells and Rebecca West. Upon hearing of her own inclusion among those to be executed, West was reported to have commented to Coward: 'My dear, the people we should have been seen dead with!'

When not travelling to entertain the troops and his fellow citizens, Coward lived in London throughout the war. After being bombed out of his London home in 1941, he went to live in the Savoy hotel for the rest of the conflict. After the war he bought a home in Jamaica, as did his friend Ian Fleming, and Coward died there in 1973. In 2006 the Albery Theatre in St Martin's Lane, Westminster was refurbished and renamed the Noel Coward Theatre in his memory.

Origins of 007
Ian Fleming takes to his naval role with zeal

M any current and future authors were attracted to the work of the secret services during World War II. Perhaps the best known of these to later generations is Ian Fleming (1908–64), author of the James Bond novels. Descended from a wealthy banking family, Fleming was educated at Eton. With the encouragement of his family, he subsequently joined a finance business in the City of London, where he did not prove to be a success. In 1939 he was recruited into the naval intelligence service, a role for which he appears to have had

no qualifications. In time he became personal assistant to its head, Rear Admiral John Godfrey, working from the Admiralty Building in Whitehall. Fleming was then commissioned into the Royal Naval Volunteer Reserve and attained the rank of commander – as did his best-known progeny, James Bond.

Fleming took to his new role with a zeal later demonstrated by his fictional character 007, devoting much of his time to devising fantastic schemes to outwit the Germans. One of his most outlandish, proposed in September 1940, was to man a German bomber brought down over England during the Battle of Britain with RAF crew dressed in Luftwaffe uniforms. In his plan, the bomber would be dropped in the English Channel, where the crew would then overpower the Germans that came to their rescue, seize their boat and Enigma coding machine, and bring them back to England. This plan was not followed up, partly on the grounds that the bomber would have sunk long before the German rescuers arrived – Bletchley Park had to wait until May 1941 for an Enigma to be captured from a U-boat by the crew of HMS *Bulldog*.

Another proposal, which Fleming described as 'not very nice', was to drop a corpse attached to a parachute that failed to open in occupied Europe, accompanied by papers designed to mislead the enemy. It is fascinating to learn that a variation of this idea was eventually adopted for the disinformation plan named Operation Mincemeat that took place towards the end of the war. In the event, a corpse was dropped into the Atlantic Ocean off the coast of Portugal with documents that convinced the Germans that the Allies would invade Greece rather than Italy.

Some of Fleming's ideas did take shape as he intended. He was involved in the recruitment and training of a special intelligence unit, which in 1943 was re-designated 30 Assault Unit, a Commando of the Royal Marines. After very rigorous training in skills such as survival and unarmed combat, this unit moved in ahead of advancing troops to work behind enemy lines, gathering intelligence, documents, equipment and captured

personnel that could help the Allied forces. Their work was so secret that little of what they did is known even now – the present author only learned of them through his late cousin, one of the Royal Marines involved.

Although Ian Fleming's wartime work was largely completed behind a desk at the Admiralty in Whitehall, there is clearly a link between the schemes he devised and the later outlandish activities of the fictional secret agent, 007. One of the best-known literary creations of the 20th century, 007 has long outlived his author, who eventually died in 1964.

Ministry of Truth
Could Brendan Bracken be Big Brother?

Like Graham Greene (see 'Sardines in a Gigantic Tin'), George Orwell also worked for the Ministry of Information in the Senate House building in Bloomsbury during World War II. But he did not get on with his boss, Minister of Information Brendan Bracken (1901–58). Of Irish origin, although not anxious to acknowledge the fact, Bracken befriended Winston Churchill when the future Prime Minister was in the political wilderness and out of Parliament. Stanley Baldwin was to refer to Bracken as Churchill's 'faithful chela', the Hindi word for a disciple; meanwhile, Bracken himself allowed others to believe, without reason, that he was Churchill's illegitimate son.

In 1929 Bracken became a Conservative Member of Parliament, and in 1941 Churchill appointed him to the position of Minister of Information, with responsibility for publicity and propaganda. In this office, which Bracken held until the

Senate House

end of the war, he showed much of the flair that later enabled him to create the modern *Financial Times* and turn it, after the war, into Europe's leading financial and business newspaper, the only serious rival to the *Wall Street Journal*.

From 1941 to 1943 George Orwell worked for the Ministry of Information as a producer of talks for the Far Eastern Service, as did his wife Eileen in the censorship department. At his interview, Orwell impressed with his acceptance of the need for propaganda against enemies such as the Germans and Japanese. However, his stern puritan nature soon rebelled, with him writing: 'All propaganda is lies, even when one is telling the truth'.

In turn, this led to his disapproval of Bracken, who had become known as 'BB'. It has been suggested that these initials were the origin of Big Brother, the fictional character and symbol of Orwell's most famous and dystopian work 1984. That work's grim Ministry of Truth, with its 'enormous pyramidal structure of glittering white concrete rising 300 metres into the air', certainly resembles the white Portland stone of London's Senate House, although the building itself, by the architect Charles Holden, only reaches 64m (210ft).

HOPELESS WITH MONEY

The many achievements of Sir Winston Churchill (1874–1965) are well known, but one fact about him is rarely mentioned: he was hopeless with money. In 1924, as Chancellor of the Exchequer in Stanley Baldwin's Conservative government, Churchill authorized a return to the gold standard. This had been abandoned during World War I, and Churchill's decision revalued the pound to a level that made British exports uncompetitive. The decision provoked the economist J M Keynes to write his polemic essay **The Economic Consequences of Mr Churchill,** *and Churchill's action helped to cause the General Strike of 1926, as well as the depression that followed.*

When Churchill entered government as First Lord of the Admiralty in 1911, his salary would not have covered his expenditure on wine and cigars. As usual friends

Winston Churchill

came to his aid, among them Brendan Bracken. With the help of friends, Churchill's expensive home at Chartwell was transferred to the National Trust and rented to Churchill for an annual rent of £350. Yet on the eve of his and his nation's finest hour in 1940, his finances were still perilous. Only after 1945, with the sales of his books and the hospitality of wealthy people seeking his company, was he freed from financial anxiety. However, even in Churchill's last years his advisers were engaged in a dispute with the Inland Revenue.

Closely guarded secrets
The government goes underground

The continuing threat of bombing during World War II obliged some crucial government matters to be conducted from premises safely buried beneath the streets of London. The best known of these are the Cabinet War Rooms, a closely guarded secret for many years but opened to the public in 1984, accessible from King Charles Street off Whitehall. Converted from a basement to government offices, they became fully operational in August 1939, just before the outbreak of war. During the conflict the Cabinet met there over 100 times, chaired either by Churchill, or in his absence by his deputy, Clement Attlee.

The centre of the complex was a map room in which vital information was collected for the Cabinet then passed on to King George VI. This information was gathered from the armed services, as well as the civil defence bodies who brought news of air raids. Ultra information from the code-breakers at Bletchley Park was also collected in this room, revealing the coded messages sent by German commanders to their military forces. It was therefore here that delicate decisions were made over which Ultra secrets should be passed on to commanders in the field, and which should not be used for fear of disclosing the sophistication of the code breakers' work.

In March 1941, Ultra learned of a plan by the Italian Mediterranean fleet to intercept an Allied convoy passing through the Suez Canal. The decision was taken in the Cabinet War Rooms to pass the information on to Admiral Andrew Cunningham, Commander-in-Chief of the Royal Navy's Mediterranean Fleet, which duly ambushed the Italian fleet and destroyed it. However to protect Ultra's secrecy, a reconnaissance plane was sent out shortly before the attack to locate the Italians 'by chance'. Incidentally, a young midshipman named Philip Mountbatten served in the battle on HMS *Valiant* – he was later to become Prince Philip, Duke of Edinburgh.

Just two months after the ambush of the Italian fleet, as the Royal Navy hunted down the fearsome German battle cruiser *Bismarck*, a Bletchley code breaker decrypted the name of the French port of Brest as the ship's destination. This was passed on and led to the destruction of the *Bismark*, but not before the ship had again been 'spotted' by aircraft. Through such decisions, made in these very rooms, the secrecy of Ultra was preserved.

BED AND BREAKFAST

Besides the map rooms and other working spaces, the Cabinet War Rooms contained a telephone room. From this, Churchill could make transatlantic telephone calls to President Roosevelt in Washington, via an encryption machine installed in the basement of Selfridge's department store in Oxford Street. There were also bedrooms for Churchill, his wife Clementine, and for Churchill's friend and Minister of Information, Brendan Bracken (see Ministry of Truth). Both Churchill and his wife usually slept in Downing Street, although their daughter Mary (later Mary Soames) often used her mother's bedroom within the complex. Today,

the site of the Cabinet War Rooms is administered by the Imperial War Museum, and the rooms may all still be seen by visitors.

Famously taciturn
Clement Attlee serves in the War Cabinet

It would be hard to imagine a greater contrast than the one between the flamboyant, orotund Prime Minister Winston Churchill and his Deputy Prime Minister in the War Cabinet, the understated, taciturn Clement Attlee (1883–1967), later Earl Attlee. Attlee was born into a prosperous middle-class household, went to Oxford and qualified as a barrister, yet he found his true vocation working among the poor in the East End of London. He worked in a Boys' Club in Stepney, and later for Toynbee Hall in Whitechapel, before becoming Mayor of Stepney in 1919 then Member of Parliament for Limehouse in 1922.

In 1935 he was elected as Leader of the Labour Party at a time when, following some poor election results,

Clement Attlee

Labour had few MPs. Despite the envy that his success provoked among some Labour colleagues such as Herbert Morrison (see Dynamic Force), he remained the party's leader for 20 years, far longer than any other politician. Besides serving in the War Cabinet during World War II, he also led the radical reforming government of 1945 to 1951, which nationalized industries left in ruins by the war.

And, of course, his government established the British National Health Service.

When Attlee chaired the Cabinet in Churchill's absence, its meetings were invariably shorter and far more sharply focussed on the agenda. Churchill liked to expand, often at great length, on matters under discussion – and others that weren't – drawing lengthy comparisons with great historical events. Churchill famously underestimated Attlee, dismissing him as 'a sheep in sheep's clothing' and 'a modest man with much to be modest about'. He paid the price for doing so when he lost the General Election of 1945 to Attlee.

Attlee was famously taciturn, never using one word where none would do the job. His modesty sometimes concealed a strong sense of his own worth and a sharp sense of humour. He composed limericks, of which one sums him up better than any statement by others:

Few thought he was even a starter
There were many who thought
   themselves smarter.

But he finished PM,
    CH and OM,
An Earl and a Knight of the Garter.

In January 1965, Attlee was a pallbearer at Churchill's funeral. After retiring, he lived with his family in Prestwood, Buckinghamshire, an area of which he had become fond while using the nearby country house retreat of Chequers during his time as Prime Minister. He died in 1967 and is buried in Westminster Abbey.

CRICKET MACHINE
Clement Attlee was not much impressed by what he regarded as new-fangled inventions, but he was devoted to cricket. When he moved into 10 Downing Street as Prime Minister, one of his advisers told him that he should have a teleprinter installed to keep him informed of breaking news. Attlee was not persuaded to do so until it was explained that the machine would transmit the latest cricket scores, whereupon he agreed.

On one occasion Attlee's press secretary, Francis Williams, briefed the lobby correspondents of the press on the results of the Cabinet's deliberations. He was later summoned to see the Prime Minister, who complained: 'There's an account of this morning's cabinet on my cricket machine!' That was in the days before spin doctors.

Dynamic force
Herbert Morrison and his impact on London

Herbert Morrison (1888–1965), later Baron Morrison, was a dynamic force in the Labour Party, in the wartime government, and above all, in the government of London. He was born in the year the Local Government Act created the London County Council and he died in the year that this council passed into history. His ashes were scattered on the Thames outside the London County Council's former headquarters, County Hall.

Born in Brixton as the son of a policeman and a maidservant, both Morrison's parents were born within the sound of the bells of St Maryle-Bow church on Cheapside and therefore qualify as Cockneys. He left school at the age of 14 to work as a grocer's errand boy for 7 shillings (£18 at today's value) a week, and in 1907 he joined the Social Democratic Federation, denouncing capitalism from soapboxes. He later joined the Labour Party where he met Clement Attlee, with whom he was to have an enduring but often uneasy relationship.

Morrison opposed World War I as a conscientious objector, working as a nurseryman at Letchworth Garden City – but he had no doubts about the need to fight World War II against the Nazis. In the 1920s he became Mayor of Hackney, and with the Mayor of Stepney, Clement Attlee, he led a delegation to Downing Street to protest about unemployment and hardship among the poor. In 1923 he became a Member of Parliament for Hackney and proceeded to transform the fortunes of the Labour Party in London, organizing debates, choirs, football, cricket and darts leagues. Indeed, he declared: 'We must not only work our way to Socialism, we must sing in the course of our journey'.

In 1929 Morrison became Minister of Transport in the Labour government of Prime Minister Ramsay Macdonald. From this position he introduced driving licences and created the London Passenger Transport Board, which covered the London Underground, buses and trams. In 1934 he became leader of the London County Council, describing London as 'a disgrace to civilisation', but later mellowed to add,

Herbert Morrison

'I love London town'. In 1940, as Germany mounted its attack on the Western Front, Morrison opened the Norway Debate in the House of Commons. This led to the fall of Prime Minister Neville Chamberlain and the appointment of Churchill's government instead.

As France collapsed, Churchill appointed him Minister of Supply, following, in Morrison's own words, 'the most discouraging interview I have ever had', as the Prime Minister outlined the dire situation that the nation faced. He was also appointed Home Secretary and Minister of Home Security, and it was in these capacities that Morrison, with the dynamic energy that marked him, organized the tube shelters and the civil defence force of air raid wardens, shelter wardens and voluntary organizations that kept London going throughout the Blitz and its aftermath.

When Labour won the 1945 Parliamentary election, Morrison attempted to supplant Clement Attlee as Prime Minister but failed, an attempt that won him the lasting hostility of Ernest Bevin.

Morrison subsequently steered Labour's nationalisation legislation through the Commons, organized the Festival of Britain in 1951, and lost to Hugh Gaitskell in the Labour Party leadership election that followed Attlee's resignation in 1955. Herbert Morrison is one of the most important figures in the history of the Labour Party, World War II, and above all of London, yet he never cast off his reputation as a conspirator. His grandson is the Labour politician Peter Mandelson.

Mickey the Midget
Taking London's shelters in hand

In the late 1930s the British government, fearful of air raids, began to seek suitable buildings for use as public air raid shelters in London and across the rest of Britain. Those with stoutly constructed basements and cellars were earmarked for the purpose, so when World War II began notices directed the population towards them. Many of these were found at schools, hospitals and business premises, meanwhile railway arches and railway goods depots were similarly singled out. In addition, a programme of shelter construction began, although this was curtailed in 1940 when bricks and concrete became required for military installations instead.

Some of the tailor-made shelters were not a success, especially those whose walls, when damaged, caused their concrete ceilings to collapse on to the helpless occupants. Haldane shelters were primarily used in London, named after the scientist J B S Haldane who had visited Spain during the Civil War. There he had studied the shelters used in Barcelona to protect the civil population against air raids by the Fascist forces, many of who were in fact Germans and Italians. Haldane shelters were erected on the surface, with concrete sides and metal roofs reinforced by metal tubes – few were built and none survive.

The most populous part of London, and the most bombed, was the East End close to the docks. The Tilbury Shelter was nearby: one of the largest shelters in London, it was created from the subterranean goods depot of Liverpool Street station. Designed to accommodate 3,000 people, on occasions in the early months of the Blitz it held up to 14,000 occupants. Meanwhile, the nearby Bethnal Green shelter in Victoria Park, suitable for about 500 people, on occasion accommodated three times that number – so many that the shelter warden was unable to penetrate the crowd to ensure people were safe.

Determined individuals took other shelters in hand, one of the most zealous being Mickey the Midget. His real name was Michael Davis and he was Deputy Mayor of Stepney, now part of the London Borough of Tower Hamlets. An optician by profession, Mickey was about 1.07m (3ft 6in) tall and took in hand the shelter in the basement of the London Fruit and Wool Exchange in Brushfield Street, Spitalfields. During the Blitz 2,500 people would crowd into this shelter, which had no sanitation, medical facilities, light or heat.

Mickey set up first aid posts and a dispensary at this shelter, and he recruited a doctor and stretcher-bearers to come to the shelter to care for the sick. At his suggestion, Marks & Spencer provided money for a canteen. Mickey purchased and distributed milk with the profits from selling food to the shelter occupants – this was distributed free to the children. When the government eventually took control of the shelter and appointed its own shelter marshal, the occupants quickly decided otherwise – thus Mickey became Mickey the Marshal.

Closer to the City of London itself, Finsbury Council proposed the construction of an underground shelter to hold 7,000 people. However Haldane observed that if a bomb fell at the entrance, the force of the blast would probably kill all the inmates. He sagely observed that the only way to be sure of the outcome was to test this fearful prospect at such a shelter – before hastily adding that he did not recommend this course of action! The council went ahead anyway with the construction of a smaller unit – the entrance to the shelter, which happily survived the war intact, may be seen in Garnault Place off Rosebery Avenue, EC1.

Attempts were made to raise the morale of those using the shelters, but these were not always well received. The novelist and wartime firewatcher Nancy Mitford went to one public shelter to talk about her work. However, her rather upper-class accent and patronizing manner so offended the bewildered occupants that she was not invited back! Others were more closely attuned to the sensibilities of the shelterers: one enterprising marshal placed a sign above the entrance that read 'Adolf's Kindergarten; no bombs here'.

Under the circumstances, it is perhaps not surprising that the great majority of Londoners preferred to remain at home and risk the bombing. Nevertheless, some shelters, such as the one in the basement of Harrods department store, were very comfortable indeed, with chairs for everyone and first aid workers on hand.

Cover at home
Mysterious Anderson and Morrison shelters

As World War II approached in the summer of 1939, some mysterious and rather clumsy objects

The Anderson shelter was the more elaborate of the two. This consisted of two sheets of corrugated iron, which, when bolted together at the top, formed a semi-circle that could be placed in a trench in the garden measuring 91cm (3ft) deep. Then the excavated material was used to cover the corrugated iron semi-circle with a 46cm (18in) layer of earth, also forming an embankment for the structure at each side and at one end. A metal plate protected each end, one of which could be moved to provide an entrance. The resulting shelters were about 2m (7ft) long, 1m (3ft) wide and 2m (7ft) high, and could sleep two people in modest comfort, or, with bunks, four people in some discomfort. The earth provided both additional protection against falling debris and also some insulation against the cold; moreover, some enterprising householders installed a sump to drain away water that penetrated the shelter.

Anderson shelter

began to appear in the homes and gardens of London, especially those close to possible enemy targets such as aerodromes. These were Anderson shelters and Morrison shelters, named after Sir John Anderson and Herbert Morrison respectively, each of who served as Home Secretary at some point during the war. Interestingly, neither of these men had anything to do with the shelters named after them. Instead, eminent civil engineers designed these for people to enjoy a reasonable degree of protection within the comfort of their own homes, thus reducing the need for public shelters.

A company that described itself as Glaziers of Savile Row advertised a superior version of this shelter in *The Times* – it is not known how or indeed whether this version was superior, since none survived the war. It was claimed that Anderson shelters would protect against anything apart from a direct bomb strike; in fact, one shelter's occupants did survive a direct hit by a crashing Messerschmitt, although the shelter itself was wrecked. The Anderson shelter was promoted by a feature on *Band Waggon* (sic), the BBC's popular entertainment show that featured the comedians Arthur Askey and Richard Murdoch. Many of the Anderson shelters survived the war as garden sheds.

The Morrison shelter was provided free to homes whose income was less than £400 per annum and was a simpler structure. Consisting of a thick metal plate that measured 2m (7ft) long and a little over 1m (3ft) wide supported by four posts, its sides were formed from wire mesh. This shelter was usually assembled over a bed, whose occupants would therefore be protected from falling debris. Your author was thus protected in his cot, and although he was only one year old at the time, he remembers the components of the shelter in his parents' garden after the

war, as a variety of uses were found for them.

It was estimated that about 1.4 million people had access to public shelters, while about 200,000 used the tube stations and tunnels as shelter each night during the Blitz. However most people, as many as 80 per cent in the London area, chose to remain at home during the air raids, preferring to risk the bombs rather than lose a night's sleep. Many of these used Anderson or Morrison shelters, which were to be found in around half the households of London.

Looking the East End in the face
West End and Buckingham Palace are bombed

In the initial stages of the Blitz during World War II, virtually all the attacks by the Luftwaffe were made on the commercial heart of the capital: the City of London itself, the East End, and above all, the docks. These areas were targeted because they were essential to London's livelihood, as food and fuel were imported through them for the war effort. As a consequence, it was the poor of London who were most affected by these bombings. Following an air raid, King George VI and Queen Elizabeth often arrived quickly on the scene, their presence alone raising the morale of the stricken populace.

Early in the war, some of the more affluent sent their wives and children to Canada or the USA, as many as 11,000 departing from London in this way. There had been some discussion of the removal of the London-based Royal Family to a place of safety in Canada, yet George VI would not hear of it. As Queen Elizabeth explained: 'The children can't go without me. I can't leave the King and of course the King won't go'. The two princesses spent much of their time at Windsor, but the king and queen remained at Buckingham Palace in the heart of London, where the king practised revolver shooting in the grounds and would have died fighting.

The embarrassment caused by the fact that the affluent areas of the West End of London were being spared finally ended when Buckingham Palace was bombed – first on 8 September 1940, and more seriously on 13 September

Buckingham Palace

while the Royal Family was in residence. One person was killed but the royals were uninjured, although messages of condolence poured into the palace from all over the world. Further raids followed over the next five days: following one of them, an unexploded bomb was removed from the palace on a stretcher. It was these developments that prompted Queen Elizabeth to write: 'I'm glad we have been bombed. It makes me feel we can look the East End in the face'.

BLINDS DRAWN

As well as the king and queen, Prime Minister Winston Churchill was assiduous in visiting victims of bombing, as was the Deputy Prime Minister, Clement Attlee. The latter was already a familiar figure in Stepney, where he had been Mayor, and Limehouse, which he represented in Parliament. By contrast, when the tables were turned and the RAF began its raids on Germany, Hitler never visited the devastated areas. As he travelled through them, his train blinds were drawn to spare him from the scenes of desolation.

Bull and Bush
Unusual uses for London Underground stations

Besides the Cabinet War Rooms (see Closely Guarded Secrets), many disused – or in one case never used – Underground stations were used for the war effort during World War II. Down Street, opposite the Piccadilly entrance to Green Park station, can be found in the heart of Mayfair, and a pedestrian walking north along it may notice an unusual building on the left. Amid the smart residences is a building whose red tiles and distinctive architecture make it look more like the entrance to an Underground station than the small shop that later occupied the premises.

This is indeed the former Down Street station, which was located between Hyde Park Corner and Green Park stations on the Piccadilly Line. It had been closed in 1932 for lack of adequate use, but was offered to the government as a refuge during World War II, where it came to be used mostly by the Railway Executive Committee, and occasionally by the War Cabinet. A brick partition was erected to screen the station from passing trains so it is no longer visible, but Transport for London is now seeking a partner to redevelop its facilities for use as offices or similar purposes.

Brompton Road, another disused Underground station, became the headquarters of London's anti-aircraft defences. Located between Knightsbridge and South Kensington stations, the building's distinctive red tiling again betrays its original use. The station building has now been sold, evidently to a Ukrainian investor, with a view to converting it for residential use in this expensive area close to Harrods department store.

However, the most unusual Underground station used during World War II lies deep beneath Hampstead Heath, but was never actually brought into use as a station. Officially named North End station and located between Hampstead and Golders Green, it is commonly known as the Bull and Bush, owing to its proximity to the pub of that name made famous in song.

North End station was built in the early 1900s, as the Northern Line – then the Charing Cross, Euston and Hampstead Railway – extended towards Edgware. However, when it became clear that no housing development would at that time be permitted on nearby Hampstead Heath, the station was neither opened nor completed. Nevertheless, its platforms are still there and now used for storing engineering materials.

North End station was brought into use for emergencies, and on 29 September 1940, it was once used, experimentally, for a Cabinet meeting – in Churchill's words 'far from the light of day'. Lying at a depth of 67m (220ft), if the station had opened it would have been the deepest of all Underground stations, a title currently held by the adjacent Hampstead station. A member of the Home Guard who was on sentry duty nearby in September 1940 reported: 'Mr Churchill popped out of the ground at my feet'.

World's longest factory
*Making fighter aircraft in
London's tunnels*

During World War II, it was important to protect the factories in and around London that made and assembled essential equipment for war effort. One of these was the Plessey factory in Ilford – then located in Essex, but now part of the London Borough of Redbridge.

When World War II began, work had stopped on the extension of the Central Line of the Underground system into Essex, leaving tunnels completed but without any railway tracks. A 5-mile section of these tunnels lay between Leytonstone and Gants Hill, and this was taken over by Plessey to become an aircraft components factory. Machinery was moved in and a single-track narrow gauge railway was temporarily installed. Trolleys ran along this track with equipment, materials and components to service what was surely the world's longest production line, boasting 27,871 sq m (300,000 sq ft) of secure space.

Most of the 2,000-strong factory workforce was female, and these women worked around the clock undisturbed by the worst air raids – they were, in effect, working in a bombproof air raid shelter. Essential components for Spitfire fighter aircraft, Halifax and Lancaster bombers, and even Churchill tanks, were produced in this factory until the end of the war. At that point, the production lines were removed from their troglodytic existence and transferred to a new factory location in Ilford. By a strange irony, the new factory was eventually sold to the German company, Siemens.

A similar but smaller scale operation was installed in the tunnel that led from Earl's Court Underground station to the district's museums. Here aircraft components were produced, the labour force consisting of London Transport staff working a spot of overtime after their main shifts. At the bus maintenance depots at Aldenham and Acton, the equipment and skilled workforce was turned over to assembling Halifax bombers, as well as to converting Sherman tanks into swimming ones. The latter were able to swim ashore on to the D-Day beaches to provide some much needed protection for the British and Canadian infantry as they stormed ashore.

Mysterious tunnels
Air raid shelters, secret bunkers or document stores?

In November 1940, Home Secretary Herbert Morrison (see A Dynamic Force) announced that 'a new system of tunnels linked to the London tubes' were to be bored. No explanation was given for this decision and the timing is strange, since by that time the London population was sleeping at home, in public shelters or in the tube stations. The mysterious and distinctive surface structures of these tunnels may still be seen, looking futuristic even by 21st-century standards.

Construction was completed by 1942, when the magazine *The Engineer* reported that: 'Eight new tube shelters in the London area are now so nearly completed that in an emergency they could be brought into use without delay. [They are] constructed in such positions that they can become part of new tube railways that may be driven beneath London when the war is over'.

Each of these tunnels was capable of sleeping 8,000 people, yet they were never used as air raid shelters. What were they for? The answer is no doubt hidden away in a classified file somewhere, however they may well have been intended as a refuge for essential government services in the event of a devastating strike on the capital. By 1940 no one held any illusions about Hitler's ruthlessness, and there were many rumours about terror weapons, germ warfare, rockets and other horrors that might have required drastic action, such as sending the government of Britain underground.

It is also probably significant that seven of these tunnels were built alongside the Northern Line stations at Clapham South, Clapham Common, Clapham North, Stockwell, Goodge Street, Camden Town and Belsize Park, with one at Chancery Lane by the Central Line. As now, during the early 20th century the Northern Line was notoriously overcrowded. So the nearby location of the Northern Line stations and the report in *The Engineer* suggests that the builders had a post-war plan in mind to connect them as a relief line for its long-suffering passengers.

If this was the case, the relief line was never built – but the tunnels remain. And although they were never used as air raid shelters, some of these tunnels did find military uses. Three of them were used

by the War Office as temporary accommodation for soldiers passing through London on their way south to the Normandy beaches. The one in Chenies Street near Goodge Street station, still a very conspicuous part of the landscape, was used for a while as Supreme Allied Commander Dwight Eisenhower's headquarters while he planned the Normandy invasion. And after D-Day it became the communications headquarters for the British and Canadian beaches of Gold, Juno and Sword, receiving the first reports of the drama as it unfolded in that historic landing. Most of the tunnels, their origins still mysterious, are now used as document stores.

EMPIRE WINDRUSH

In June 1948, the passenger liner **Empire Windrush** *approached Tilbury on the Thames with the first immigrants from the West Indies. Some of these were men who had served in the British armed forces during World War II and were returning to what they regarded as the mother country. Initial wild*

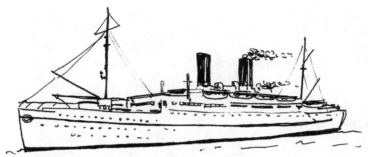

Empire Windrush

talk about sending a destroyer to turn them back to the West Indies subsided. Then the suggestion that these immigrants would not survive the British winter provoked the observation that they had survived the wartime winters, so why not the peacetime ones, too?

Eventually an RAF policeman named Baron Baker was sent to meet the ship and accommodation was provided for the new arrivals at the Clapham Common shelter. In the days that followed, the residents made their way to the Labour Exchange on Coldharbour Lane in Brixton – in this way the Afro-Caribbean community of Brixton was born. In 1951 the wartime air

raid shelters across London were used to house visitors to the Festival of Britain, many of them boy scouts from around the Commonwealth.

Evacuating London
Citizens escape by train, bus and boat

Of course, the safest way to escape London's bombs was to leave the capital for safer locations in villages and small towns around the country. On 1 September 1939, as the Nazis attacked Poland, the Vice Chairman of London Transport, Frank Pick, travelled from his home in Hampstead Garden Suburb to

Oakland station on the Piccadilly Line in order to supervise his plan for the evacuation of London's children from the city.

Pick had arranged for about half a million children to be taken by underground trains to outlying mainline stations in order to avoid overcrowding the London Terminus stations. In addition, about a quarter of a million were conveyed to stations on buses, some drivers working continuously for 36 hours. The evacuation of school age children, accompanied by teachers, was organized by the London County Council; younger children were accompanied by volunteers from the Women's Voluntary Service. Each child bore a name badge and clutched a gas mask and a package of belongings, including teddy bears and other favourite toys. On the day, two babies were observed tied by a strap to a large suitcase, as their parents went in search of information. Meanwhile

Evacuee

children from Dagenham were evacuated by boat to East Anglia.

At Oakland station, Pick surveyed a portion of the children transferring to several of the 2,000 mainline trains that would carry them away from London and danger. Then he journeyed to his office at 55 Broadway to check that the plan was running smoothly elsewhere – it was. He never doubted that the war would be won, writing to one of his young assistants: 'The war may shake our stability and daunt our ambition but a good peace will, with time, restore us and London to a better, finer, decenter basis'. This was a widely held view among the population of London as a whole, and it would remain unshaken, despite setbacks, in the years ahead.

In addition to the population, many organizations were also evacuated from London. An insurance company was moved from the city to Newland Park, a stately home near Chalfont St Giles. After the war, the 'temporary' buildings constructed to accommodate this company were used to accommodate students of a teacher training college until the 1980s. By December 1939, a total of 3,500 firms had left London in this way, together with schools and universities.

The London School of Economics moved from its London home in Houghton Street to Cambridge. Its famous economist Friedrich Hayek moved with the university, his views on economics at odds with those of his great Cambridge contemporary, John Maynard Keynes. It followed that on occasion the two men did fire-watching duties on the roof of King's College Chapel in Cambridge. There were no bombs or fires, but there must have been some interesting conversations!

'THAT IMPECCABLE BUSMAN'

Besides his work in organizing the evacuation of children from London and in finding a model for WVS recruitment (see German Model), Frank Pick was moved to the Ministry of Information. Here he expressed misgivings about the Prime Minister's plan to drop leaflets over Germany to spread false information. In late 1940, Pick was summoned to see the great man at a meeting of the Political Warfare Executive where the following brief conversation took place:

Churchill: *Now Mr Pick I understand that you have been objecting to the dropping of the leaflets.*

Pick: *Yes, Prime Minister, what is written on the leaflets is not wholly true and that is bad propaganda.*

Churchill: *This is no time to be concerned with the niceties.*

Pick: *Prime Minister, I have never told a lie in my life.*

Churchill: *Mr Pick, yesterday the Germans shelled Dover with their long-range guns at Cape Gris Nez. This afternoon I shall be visiting Dover. I may be killed by a German shell. If so, it will be a great comfort to me to know that on the last day of my life I spoke with*

*a man who had never told a
lie in his life. Get out!*

*As Pick left the room, Churchill
turned to his secretary John Colville.
In a deafening whisper, he instructed
'Never let that impeccable busman
darken my door again'. Pick left the
Ministry and died the following year
of a brain haemorrhage.*

'Patron of our age'
*Frank Pick, connoisseur of
modern design*

Frank Pick (1878–1941) may have
fallen out with Winston Churchill
(see 'That Impeccable Busman')
but he was nevertheless a seminal
figure in London life as World War
II approached – not only in creating
the evacuation plan (see Evacuating
London). Born in Lincolnshire, in
1928 he became Managing Director
of the Underground Group. Here
he was responsible for the network
extensions out towards Cockfosters
on the Piccadilly Line, and to
Roding Valley and Epping on the
Central Line. Part of the latter was

later used to form the Leytonstone
to Gants Hill subterranean aircraft
components factory (see World's
Longest Factory).

A shy and reserved man, Pick was
also a connoisseur and enthusiastic
advocate of modern design. The
architectural historian Nikolaus
Pevsner described him as 'the greatest
patron of the arts whom this century
has so far produced in England
and indeed the ideal patron of our
age'. Pick engaged the services of
the Art Nouveau architect Charles
Holden to design eight stations on
the Piccadilly Line, five of which
are now listed buildings. Indeed,
Pevsner singled out one of them, the
Bauhaus-style Arnos Grove, for its
'repose and dignity'.

Pick also commissioned the
architect Holden to design the
headquarters of the Underground
Group at 55 Broadway, SW1. At
the time this was completed in
1929, decorated with controversial
sculptures by Jacob Epstein, it
was the tallest office building in
London. He then commissioned the
early work of artists such as Mabel
Lucie Attwell, Paul Nash, Graham

Sutherland and McKnight Kauffer, which appeared in poster designs for the London Underground. Later in 1944 London transport commissioned a series of memorable posters entitled *The Proud City* by Walter Spradbery, which depicted famous London buildings rising above the devastation.

BEST INVESTMENT

Perhaps Frank Pick's most conspicuous legacy was his decision, after some hesitation, to authorize the production of the famous London Tube map. Harry Beck was the designer of this icon of industrial design, at the time an unemployed electrical draughtsman. Pick bought the copyright of the design from Beck for 5 guineas (£125 at today's value), surely the best investment he ever made for an image that is now reproduced on everything from clothing and crockery to wallpaper and mouse mats.

Phoney war
Followed by the evacuation from Dunkirk

The first air raid warning sounded from one of the 2,000 sirens posted around the capital soon after Prime Minister Neville Chamberlain solemnly announced from Downing Street that Britain was 'at war with Germany'. People scurried to the Whitehall air raid shelters, only to learn that it was a false alarm. Over the next eight months of what became known as the 'phoney war' there were few causes for alarm in the capital. The Luftwaffe was occupied with defeating Poland and too busy to concern itself with Britain. Even when the German army invaded Belgium, Holland, Luxembourg and France on 10 May 1940, there was no fear that there would be a collapse in the West. It was only after the evacuations from Dunkirk between 27 May and 4 June 1940 that the threat to Britain and its capital became real.

During this period, against all odds and contrary to most expectations, over 330,000 British and Allied troops were rescued from the beaches of Dunkirk in the face of German attacks as France fell. The evacuation was code-named Operation Dynamo, and the legend of the 'little ships' that took part in the rescue remains one of the most heroic episodes of World War II. London made a special contribution to the endeavour. Two ships, the *Royal Sovereign* and *Royal Daffodil*, were usually employed in carrying people on pleasure trips from Tower Pier in London to Southend, Margate, and occasionally across to France. Having been used to evacuate children from London to East Anglia at the start of the war (see Evacuating London), they later joined the fleet that rescued troops from the Dunkirk beaches. After the war they returned to their peacetime roles, meanwhile their contribution to this great evacuation was recorded on brass plates upon their decks.

Back and forth
London evacuated under repeated threats

During the phoney war (see Phoney War), many of the people and organizations that had moved out of the capital moved back (see also Evacuating London). This meant that by the end of October 1939, 50,000 citizens, mostly children, had returned to their London homes; by November, the figure had reached 100,000; and by January 1940, 200,000 children were back in the capital. Naturally they needed to return to school for the new spring term, despite the fact that only 15 of the London County Council's schools were now open for business. By the time the Germans launched their offensive in the West, this number had doubled again to 400,000. Smiling children returned to their relieved families, one little boy commenting that his pet cat met him at the garden gate.

Also by this time around 700, a fifth, of the previously evacuated firms had returned to London. They were accompanied by the London School of Economics, which was back in its home at Houghton Street – but not for long. Once the aerial Battle of Britain over London and the South East began, followed by the Blitz bombing, the exile began again, although this time in smaller numbers. Later in 1944 the evacuation exercise was repeated yet again, when the V–1 'doodlebugs' and V–2 rockets began to attack the capital.

In effect, V–1s were pilotless aircraft full of explosives. They were launched from the continent with enough fuel to carry them to Britain, preferably London, before crashing on the capital. Their engines would cut out, and anyone in the vicinity who heard would hope the V–1 landed elsewhere – preferably in a field, as many did. The first was launched on 13 June 1944, a week after D–Day. However George Orwell, writing six months earlier, had referred to rumours of rocket guns and also of a 400-ton bomb that would be made in the form of a huge glider, which would be towed across the channel and released over London. Happily the latter dire prospect proved to be unfounded, but Orwell's 'rocket guns' did materialize in the form of doodlebugs and their successors, the V–2s.

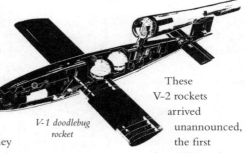

V-1 doodlebug rocket

These V–2 rockets arrived unannounced, the first striking Chiswick in London on 8 September 1944. At first the British government suppressed information about these fearsome weapons, attributing them to events such as gas explosions. However, when their true origin became known, they prompted another flight to the countryside and the shelters. This lasted only until the Allied forces overran the V–2 launch sites, as they advanced through Europe into the heartland of Germany.

FACT AND FICTION

Some London evacuees to the country prospered from their experience. Many of them had never seen farm animals, or eaten good fresh food – these children benefited greatly. One group of evacuees spent the war in the idyllic Lake District village of Grasmere where Wordsworth had lived. Meanwhile one little boy, the son of a London dustman, stayed with a middle-class family in the West Country. Here he experienced a completely different way of life, which inspired him, when he did return to London, to study hard – he eventually became the head of a major London finance house.

Other evacuees were less fortunate, and often unwanted. Indeed one local magnate arranged for the Home Guard to deposit all its rifles and ammunition in his mansion, reasoning that the billeting officer would choose not to assign evacuees to a building filled with weapons. The most notorious evacuees were Evelyn Waugh's fictional Connollys, a family of three children that he depicted in his 1942 novel, **Put Out More Flags.** *They were so horrible that the novel's billeting officer, Basil Seal, used them to extract bribes from families anxious to be rid of them.*

Attendant inconveniences
London blackout proves unpopular

During World War II, a blackout was imposed on London to ensure that no lights visible to aircraft would reveal the whereabouts of the capital. So after dark, all lights within buildings had to be switched off, or windows had to be obscured to prevent any light from being seen outside. Streetlights also had to be turned off, and even emergency vehicles such as ambulances used dimmed lights, causing several traffic accidents.

The blackout's attendant inconveniences were very unpopular, with complaints about the time it took to blackout houses every evening and absurd rumours about the lights of cigarettes being visible from 3,000m (10,000ft) above the ground. A Swiss resident of Kensington was denounced for puffing hard on a cigar then pointing the glowing end at the sky. The complainant omitted to mention that there was no air raid at the time, or that if seen the Swiss smoker would have only succeeded in bringing the wrath of the Luftwaffe upon his own head.

Heroic deeds
London's ARP wardens on the frontline

Almost 50 years after they were first made, the repeats of the BBC's *Dad's Army* still record the heroic exploits of the fictional Walmington-on-Sea Home Guard that operated under Captain George Mainwaring during World War II. Those who still enjoy this comedy will recall the regular, irritating and intrusive presence of Chief Air Raid Precaution (ARP) Warden Hodges, who was always searching for illegal lights left on during the blackout (see Attendant Inconveniences). This was when he was not engaged in arguing with Mainwaring or chatting up Mavis, the mother of Private Pike and mistress of Sergeant Wilson. Hodges thus brought a bad name to the ARP, a service that actually performed heroic deeds during the Blitz.

As it turned out, the plan to deal with the expected hordes of casualties placed the ARP wardens at the forefront of the battle during the Blitz. More important, dangerous and demanding than ensuring that people extinguished their lights was

ARP warden

the responsibility of the ARP wardens to visit bombed areas, informing the fire, police and ambulance services where the casualties had occurred and helping to rescue them. The wardens, accompanied by the Home Guard, were the front line, often acting as nurses, and occasionally as midwives, for which roles they received rudimentary training. Most fires were extinguished by the Auxiliary Fire Service (AFS), many of them women, who outnumbered the fully trained firefighters tenfold.

'Clear Hospitals'
London's hospitals adopt
wartime protocol

Contrary to earlier expectations, devastating damage to London property during World War II often caused surprisingly few casualties, a testimony to the effectiveness of the shelters referred to elsewhere in this volume. The writer Richie Calder, in his account of the Blitz entitled *Carry on London*, describes an incident in West Ham. The area had been particularly badly bombed, leaving several acres of housing ruined by bombs aimed at the London docks. Yet the only casualty was an elderly man: when advised to enter a public shelter, he had replied 'F… Jerry, I'm going to sleep in my own bed'. He was rescued with superficial injuries.

After the heroic acts of the ARP wardens (see Heroic Deeds), when dealing with London's wartime casualties the next line of defence were ambulances and specially equipped Ford and Bedford vans. Each was manned by a doctor, a nurse and up to 18 auxiliary volunteers who had received some medical training. This team would administer any feasible first aid then transfer the injured to one of ten major hospitals in inner London – among them Guy's, St Thomas's, St Bartholomew's, St Mary's, St George's and Charing Cross. These were designated as Casualty Clearing Stations, using terminology borrowed from the military and used during World War I. There the more seriously injured would be treated before being despatched to the final ring of hospitals in outer London and beyond – again using military parlance, these were described as Base Hospitals.

On the one occasion that Guy's Hospital in Southwark received the fateful telegram with the previously agreed and fateful words 'Clear Hospitals', the patients were immediately evacuated to Brighton together with most of the staff. This left behind a skeleton staff of doctors and nurses to await the anticipated floods of bombing casualties. A company of soldiers from the Queen's Regiment was posted at Guy's to deal with the riots that were anticipated when a panic-stricken population, terrified by the bombing, were expected to storm the hospital. The skeleton staff that remained behind must have felt doomed, although in fact the bombing casualties during the first months of the war were nil – even in the worst days of the Blitz they did not approach the levels feared. Eventually something like normal life returned to the hospitals in the centre of London.

Increasingly irritating
Billy Brown offers Londoners advice

One of the most conspicuous but least loved fictional characters in London during World War II was that of Billy Brown of London Town. He was a creation of David Langdon (1914–2011), who worked in the architect's department of the London County Council. Langdon drew a series of cartoons of the imaginary Billy, a City gent with a bowler hat, pinstripe suit and umbrella. Billy's appearance in posters on the London Underground, urging his fellow citizens to greater acts of responsibility and selflessness, became increasingly irritating to his fellow citizens as the war years passed.

His advice covered a variety of topics, an early one being the blackout:

Billy Brown's own highway code
For blackouts is 'Stay off the road'.
He'll never step out and begin
To meet a bus that's pulling in.
He doesn't wave his torch at night,
But 'flags' his bus with
    something white.
He never jostles in a queue
But waits and takes his turn. Do you?

Billy also plied travellers on the Underground with advice, his rhyme being headed 'To-day's Good Deed':

When you travel to and fro
On a line you really know,
Remember those who aren't
   so sure,
And haven't been that way before.
Do your good deed for the day
Tell them the stations on the way.

It was not clear how one would recognize the newcomer in need of Billy's advice. Such injunctions eventually led a reader of the *Daily Mail* to offer his own advice for Billy himself:

Some day pretty soon, by heck,
Billy Brown, I'll wring your neck.

Thus did Billy Brown pass from the history of London.

Owing it all to Hitler
Popular wartime entertainment

With the onset of World War II, the British government ordered the closure of cinemas and theatres across London and the rest of Britain, probably due to a fear that such concentrated gatherings of people might result in mass bombing casualties. The Irish playwright George Bernard Shaw described this act as 'a masterstroke of unimaginative stupidity', but many theatre and cinema owners were relieved because audiences had become so thin in the lead up to the war.

However, the regulations were soon relaxed and audiences swiftly recovered. In April 1940 the film *Gone with the Wind*, with its blend of nostalgic memories of the southern states of America and the violence of the Civil War that changed the

Film camera

South forever, proved a box office hit that ran for four years. *The Wizard of Oz* soon followed, whose escapist fantasies were enjoyed by a population suffering the privations of war.

In 1940 Winston Churchill watched *French Without Tears*, a film based on a play by Terence Rattigan. He enjoyed it so much that he arranged for the release of the young playwright Rattigan from his duties as a rear gunner in the RAF, believing that his creative works would be good for the population's morale. The result was the 1945 film *The Way to the Stars*, an account of the ordeals and triumphs of young RAF pilots during the war, as well as their relationships with their American allies. The film starred the young John Mills, Michael Redgrave and Trevor Howard.

More overtly patriotic films included the very moving *The First of the Few*, an account of the life and premature death of R J Mitchell, the designer of the Spitfire aircraft. Also *In Which We Serve*, a barely disguised account of the naval exploits of Lord Louis Mountbatten, written by his friend Noel Coward. One of the most influential war films, especially in the

USA, was *Mrs Miniver,* which starred Greer Garson as a stoical English housewife suffering the privations of war. Made in the USA, it won six Oscars and was released in 1942, strengthening American support for the struggles of the British.

In the final year of World War II, Laurence Olivier's production of Shakespeare's *Henry V* struck a resolutely patriotic note with its account of English triumph at the Battle of Agincourt in the face of overwhelming odds – admittedly against Britain's French allies on that occasion! Although, by the time the film was screened in 1945, the odds had moved decisively in the Allies' favour. All of these films, and many others, attracted large and appreciative audiences in the capital and elsewhere.

One of the successes to emerge in the world of theatre during World War II was The Windmill theatre, situated off Shaftesbury Avenue in the heart of London's entertainment district. After the brief period of compulsory closure at the start of the war, it remained open during the worst of the Blitz, thus prompting its boast 'We never closed'. Its distinctive offerings were *tableaux vivants*, literally 'living pictures', of posed naked women, which depicted spectacles such as Red Indians or Britannia ruling the waves. These were based on those at the Folies Bergères at the Moulin Rouge in Paris, but with one major difference. The Lord Chamberlain, who had been responsible for approving and censoring theatrical productions since 1737 (and continued to do so until 1968), reasoned that since there was no moral objection to nude statues in art there could also be none to nudes on stage – provided that, like statues, they didn't move. This *tableaux* formula proved to be a great success, not least among young servicemen. The Windmill also launched the careers of a number of performers who later became household names: Tony Hancock, Bruce Forsyth, Peter Sellers and Tommy Cooper were among them.

Elsewhere, risqué jokes told by Max Miller with his loud suits and rakish hat in a review named *Haw Haw!*, and Bud Flanagan and Chesney Allen in the review *Hi-De-Hi* also attracted large audiences. One of the producers who flourished during World War II was Binkie Beaumont. Born Hughes Morgan, he produced a number of classic plays, including *Hamlet* with John Gielgud and *The Importance of Being Earnest* with Gielgud and Edith Evans. Of his 59 West End productions, 52 were a success – in his own words, 'I owe it all to Hitler'.

HURRAH FOR STALIN!

One of the most marked features of film audiences during World War II was their enthusiastic reaction to the newsreels that preceded the main feature. Inevitably, much of the

Joseph Stalin

material was devoted to news of the war. Indeed any reference to British triumphs, or the screen appearance of prominent personalities such as General Bernard Montgomery, would be met with wild cheering from the crowds, while any reference to Hitler, Mussolini or their cronies provoked furious boos. Enthusiastic applause also greeted the appearance on screen of Stalin and the other Russian leaders. For the duration of the war British reserve was in abeyance, as was hostility to our gallant Communist allies.

Mass audience
The BBC comes of age

World War II is often regarded as the heroic age of the BBC, which broadcast from London to Britain and the rest of the world throughout this period. Apart from broadcasts to Europe, heard in secret by listeners in countries occupied by the Germans, the BBC was also used to transmit coded messages to resistance groups, especially during the period leading up to D-Day in 1944. But for the first time the BBC also attracted a mass audience in Britain itself, introducing a number of programmes that continued to flourish long after the war – and at least one that survives into the 21st century.

In the early days of the war, the BBC news bulletins were a main source of information on progress in the war. After the fall of France, many tuned in to Churchill's broadcasts that urged resistance 'whatever the cost'. The BBC also helped to launch the careers of stars such as Vera Lynn, 'the forces' sweetheart', although she had already appeared on stage at the London Palladium. Her song 'We'll Meet Again' has proved the most enduring one of World War II.

Meanwhile, the daytime programme *Music While You Work* was another musical offering, this time aimed at factory workers. Transmitted live, dance orchestras, military bands and brass bands played relentlessly cheerful music with strong rhythms to keep listeners working hard and fast at often repetitive tasks, such as filling shells with explosives or turning out aircraft parts for bombers and fighters. *Music While You Work* was first broadcast on the BBC in 1940 and remained on air until 1967. The song 'Deep in the Heart of Texas' proved a hit on the show, but was eventually banned because listeners were tempted to put down their tools and clap along to its rhythm at the ends of certain lines.

However, the most popular wartime programme on the BBC was *It's That Man Again*, commonly known as *ITMA*, an unflattering reference to the endless stories about Hitler that occupied news bulletins. The expression was first used in the *Daily Express*, but was then adopted by the comedian Tommy Handley in this comedy programme. It attracted unsurpassed audiences of 20 million listeners, including the Royal Family – in the words of George VI, 'We always listen'.

Often referring to current events, the episodes portrayed Tommy himself in a series of bizarre roles, such as Minister of Aggravation and Mysteries, or Governor of a South Sea island. In these, he worked with a number of eccentric characters that became associated with certain opening lines – essentially the first catchphrases. Thus Colonel Chinstrap, always looking for a drink and played by Jack Train, would never lose an opportunity to say 'I don't mind if I do', in the hope that his listener would take the hint and supply a beverage. Then the depressed Mona Lott, played by Joan Harben, sister of the first television chef Philip Harben, would gloomily proclaim 'It's being so cheerful as keeps me going'. Meanwhile Mrs Mopp, the charwoman played by Dorothy Summers, would announce her arrival at the Handley residence with 'Can I do you now, Sir?' There were many other catchphrases, but these are ones that have endured. Tommy Handley died in 1949.

Finally, the BBC's *Children's Hour*, its service for children from 5pm to 6pm each evening, had originally been broadcast from Birmingham since the earliest days. But at the beginning of the war it was transferred to the BBC Home Service in London, now Radio Four, where it remained a regular feature of the network until 1964.

STILL GOING STRONG

Desert Island Discs, *the BBC's longest-running programme, was launched during World War II in 1942, devised by broadcaster Roy Plomley (1914–85). The first guest Plomley invited to choose eight 'gramophone records' to accompany him to a desert island was the comedian Vic Oliver.*

Actually born Victor Oliver von Samek, (1898–1964), Oliver was of aristocratic Austrian birth, had served in the Austrian cavalry in World War I, yet had subsequently settled in Britain – as a Jew he was on the Nazis' blacklist. While still married to his first wife, in 1936 he became engaged to Sarah Churchill, the daughter of the future Prime Minister Winston Churchill. Churchill disapproved of Oliver, on one occasion remarking that he admired Mussolini because the Italian leader had shot his son-in-law.

Subsequent wartime guests on **Desert Island Discs** *included Guy Gibson, who had led the Dam Busters on their spectacular and perilous attack on the Ruhr Dams in 1943. Gibson was later killed on another wartime raid, but his death was not immediately revealed for fear of harming morale.* **Desert Island Discs** *continues to be broadcast to this day, now approaching its 75th birthday.*

Guy Gibson

Philosophy and health
BBC wartime information broadcasts

One of the surprises of the BBC during World War II was the popularity of the informative radio programme *The Brains Trust*, broadcast from London. Twelve million listeners tuned in to hear contributors such as 'Professor' C E M Joad, Julian Huxley and Evelyn Waugh discussing matters that ranged from abstract philosophical questions, such as the meaning of life, to more earthy matters, such as how a fly can land on a ceiling. First broadcast in January 1941 as *Any Questions?*, this name was soon changed to the one by which it is remembered – it continued as *The Brains Trust* until 1949, transferring to television in the 1950s.

During the war, the BBC radio health show *The Radio Doctor* attracted an even larger audience of 14 million to hear advice on the importance of regular bowel movements and the condition of a tongue as an indication of health. Broadcasts started in 1942, before the National Health Service was established and at a time when many people could rarely afford to see a doctor. Because doctors were not allowed to advertise, the medically trained speaker remained anonymous during the shows – he was later revealed to be Dr Charles Hill.

FALL FROM GRACE

'Professor' C E M Joad (1891–1953), one of the regular contributors to **The Brains Trust**, *suffered a fall from grace. After studying at Oxford University, he gained a reputation as someone who could clearly explain philosophical ideas. He therefore practised this skill at Birkbeck College, London, where his reputation grew although he was never actually appointed as a professor. He was also well known as a Fabian Socialist, and less well known as a serial adulterer.*

The Brains Trust *on the BBC made him a household name, yet despite his socialism he once boasted in print that he never lost an opportunity to cheat the railways. When he put this boast into practice, by travelling without a ticket from London Waterloo to Exeter, he was fined £2 and dismissed by the BBC, his reputation in ruins.*

Asserting 'eternal values'
Concerts at the National Gallery

Concerns of high culture were not confined to the BBC during World War II. At the outset of the conflict, all the paintings were removed from the National Gallery in Trafalgar Square for safe storage in a slate quarry in Wales. This left the building empty, but facing the prospect of being used as a government office.

It was spared this fate when the pianist Myra Hess approached the Director of the National Gallery, Kenneth Clark, soon after the outbreak of war to suggest that the building was used for lunchtime concerts. This idea was immediately embraced, Clark writing: 'I was delighted at the thought of the gallery being used again for its true purpose, the enjoyment of beauty, rather than for the filling in of forms or the sticking up of envelopes'.

The first concert took place at the gallery on 10 October 1939, with a 1-shilling admission charge. There was some anxiety on the part of Myra Hess that 'it would be a flop', but her

National Gallery

fears proved groundless. When the organizers opened the doors of the National Gallery ten minutes before the concert was due to start, the queue stretched out of sight. At seeing this, one of the staff exclaimed: 'We've got a problem. There are a thousand people on the pavement'. As a result, many were turned away.

During that first concert Myra Hess played Bach's *Jesu, Joy of Man's Desiring*, reducing Director Clark to tears, who exclaimed: 'This is what we have been waiting for – an assertion of eternal values'. Queen Elizabeth, herself a pianist, attended two weeks later and on many subsequent occasions, sitting among the audience. A further 1,700 performances followed, 150 of them given by Myra Hess herself along with other contributors, including the pianist Moura Lympany.

POETRY READINGS

However, poetry readings at the Aeolian Hall in New Bond Street, now occupied by Sotheby's, did not prove such a success. One, which was attended by Queen Elizabeth and her daughters Elizabeth and Margaret, heard T S Eliot read from 'The Wasteland', followed by John Masefield and Edith Sitwell. Sadly the last reader, Walter Turner, was inaudible, went beyond his allotted time, and was heckled, to the great amusement of the two princesses. As far we know, there were no further royal visits to these readings.

Paternoster Row hit
Over 5 million books destroyed

At the beginning of World War II the prospects for publishers looked bleak, with libraries in London briefly deserted. However, as the initial anxieties over the danger of bombing subsided, readers soon returned, with Foyles reporting a strong demand for novels by Trollope, Dickens and Thackeray. This trend was reflected in borrowings from the public libraries of the East End of London, with West Ham reporting that Trollope's *The Warden* and *Barchester Towers* were particularly popular with its borrowers, while Bethnal Green recorded a preference among its borrowers for the novels of Dickens.

There was a brief flurry of demand for Hitler's autobiography *Mein Kampf*, translating as 'my struggle', presumably because people were curious to know what motivated this odd human being. Yet those who have been compelled for reasons of study to read its turgid platitudes will not be surprised to learn that this demand was short lived. Unsurprisingly, there was also a very strong demand in both London's libraries and bookshops for books on gardening, cookery and do-it-yourself, as the reality of rationing and the need to erect shelters and repair bomb damage with limited materials made itself felt.

St Paul's Cathedral

Mobile Blitz libraries were set up in vans that could travel from one air raid shelter to another across the city on the worst days of the onslaught, when libraries were bombed or people were unable to travel to them. However paper shortages and consequent rationing made it hard for publishers to reprint popular titles. Disaster followed when the great firebombing raid of 29 December 1940 devastated the area around St Paul's Cathedral.

Now Paternoster Square, Paternoster Row to the north-west of the cathedral had been the home of British publishing since the early 19th century, with many leading publishers' warehouses located there. In what became known as the second great fire of London (after that of 1666), it was estimated that 5 million books were destroyed during the 29 December attack. After this, long-established magazines such as the *London Mercury, Cornhill* and *Criterion* ceased publication, some never re-appearing again.

WHAT IF?

Churchill read Hitler's autobiography **Mein Kampf** *in the 1930s, referring to it in an article he wrote in 1935. It is less well known that Churchill nearly met Hitler in 1932, shortly before Hitler came to power in Germany the following year. Churchill had been visiting Germany to see the battlefields of his great ancestor, the Duke of Marlborough; his son, Randolph Churchill, was in Germany at the same time. Randolph contacted Hitler's press secretary to arrange a meeting between the two men: one, Hitler, shortly to attain power, while the other, Churchill, was virtually ostracized at the time by the British political establishment. However, there was no response from Hitler. If the meeting had taken place, what would the two men have made of each other? Churchill had been impressed when he met Mussolini, although he soon changed his mind. This must surely be one of the great 'What Ifs?' of history.*

Mein Kampf

Obvious exception
Evelyn Waugh and other wartime literature

As London publishers began to recover from the bombing of Paternoster Row (see Paternoster Row Hit), some newer book titles started to develop a following. However, the wartime paper shortage curtailed their success, as it was rarely possible to reprint in large quantities the most popular titles. One of these, the novel *For Whom the Bell Tolls* by Ernest Hemingway, recounted the experiences of a young American volunteer in the International Brigade during the recent Spanish Civil War. Meanwhile, Margaret Mitchell's novel *Gone with the Wind* was also popular, following the success of the film released in 1940 that starred Clark Gable and Vivien Leigh.

Despite the shortages, paper was made available to new publishers during the war. So the literary critic Cyril Connolly (1903–74) took advantage of this to launch an unapologetically intellectual magazine entitled *Horizon*, which he edited from its inception in 1940 through to 1949. This magazine had a small circulation of less than 10,000 copies, yet it influenced, and in some cases published, a breed of new writers. It is interesting to learn that Sonia Brownell was associated with *Horizon* and Connolly, meeting George Orwell through the magazine and later marrying him.

Furthermore, *Horizon* magazine published the short satirical novel *The Loved One* by Evelyn Waugh

Evelyn Waugh

(1903–66), by that time already a well-known writer. Waugh's rather troubled relationship with Connolly was reflected in the author's account of the character Everard Spruce in the final volume of his war novel, *Unconditional Surrender*. Like Connolly, Spruce was editor of a highbrow literary magazine, appreciated good food and wine – which he could ill afford – and surrounded himself with attractive and well-connected young ladies.

In the same book Waugh included a sinister character named Ludovic, whose pretentious *Pensées* earned him a fortune – these platitudinous aphorisms were based upon some of Connolly's sayings.

Apart from journalism by writers like Orwell, little writing of enduring quality was inspired during World War II. The obvious exception is the output of Evelyn Waugh, three of his works owing something to his wartime experiences. His sixth novel entitled *Put Out More Flags* (1942) is an account of tragic and farcical events in the phoney war (see Phoney War). Dedicated to Waugh's friend (and occasional enemy) Randolph Churchill, the son of the Prime Minister, it has a reference to 'that odd, dead period before the Churchillian renaissance which people called at the time the Great Bore War'.

Waugh was given leave from the army to write *Brideshead Revisited*, which was published in 1945. In his own words, the novel owes something to nostalgia during 'the period of soya beans and basic English', as a result of which the book was 'infused with a kind of gluttony'. He appears to have feared that these qualities would lose him esteem among readers, but it has in fact proved to be one of his most enduringly popular books. Indeed, it has subsequently been made into both a successful television series and later a film.

Finally, the novels of Waugh's *Sword of Honour* trilogy – *Men at Arms, Officers and Gentleman* and *Unconditional Surrender* – are based loosely on Waugh's wartime experiences. The first volume, *Men at Arms* (1952), describes the difficulty experienced by Guy Crouchback, its principal character, in joining up, a reflection of Waugh's own experiences before he was accepted by the Royal Marines. Evelyn Waugh's great friend and contemporary Graham Greene never wrote a 'war novel' as such, although his later wartime experience of working as an intelligence officer in Sierra Leone informed his bleak novel *The Heart of the Matter*, which was published in 1948.

PARSNIP AND PIMPERNEL

Not all writers chose to follow the paths of Evelyn Waugh and Graham Greene in serving the war effort. The poet W H Auden and his companion Christopher Isherwood moved to the USA in 1939. They remained there throughout the conflict, for which they were widely criticized. Waugh also caricatured them in his novel Put Out More Flags, *in an imaginary conversation with Poppet, a female literary hanger-on, as Parsnip and Pimpernel, 'two great poets of her acquaintance who had recently fled to New York'.*

Publishing success
Penguin revolutionizes paperbacks

One of the great publishing successes of the war years was the well-known London publishing house, Penguin Books. Founded in 1935 by Allen Lane, with its offices from 1937 at Harmondworth in the London Borough of Hillingdon, from 1939 Penguin revolutionized the market with its paperbacks that aimed to offer the mass market quality books at affordable prices. Previously, paperbacks had been of a poor quality, but the new imprint emphasized high quality production values, as well as imaginative cover design where different colours signified the different publishing genres: orange for general fiction, green for crime fiction, and so on.

Penguin quickly took advantage of the exigencies of war with titles such as *Keeping Poultry and Rabbits on Scraps* and *Aircraft Recognition*. This ensured that their sales for the year were high, in turn ensuring the generous allocation of paper the company received in the following years during rationing. Indeed, the small page size of their books enabled Penguin to make excellent use of the paper ration they were subsequently allocated. Furthermore, they made a deal with the Canadian government to publish special editions for the Canadian armed forces, for which the company was paid in paper. Penguin also published special editions for the British forces, and a message on each book encouraged those who had read it to leave it at a post office where it could be picked up by others.

By such means, Penguin published 600 titles during World War II. As well as novels, many of these were Penguin Specials, books on current affairs that included *What Hitler Wants, Why Britain is at War* and *The Rights of Man* by H G Wells. These works were often very short, which enabled more of them to be printed from the paper ration. In January 1942, this led George Orwell to comment on the prevalence of such short books, one of them entitled *Why I Write* and written by Orwell himself. The widespread circulation of these Penguin Specials among military personnel was credited with developing a greater degree of social awareness among them, which may well have helped to secure Labour's election to government in 1945. Nevertheless, Orwell estimated that in 1945 British expenditure on tobacco was 24 times that on books, and expenditure on alcohol 30 times.

READING PLEASURE

As an experiment in 1943, many US publishers collaborated to distribute books free of charge to US forces, both at home and overseas. Altogether almost 123 million copies of books of every kind, from humorous titles to poetry and classics, were sent to US servicemen throughout the world. Many of these found their way into the hands of the Londoners who had befriended their US allies.

In the absence of many other forms of entertainment, through these books members of the US military personnel learned the pleasures of reading, which many of them continued after the conflict ended. One of their favourite titles was The Robe by Lloyd C Douglas, the story of a Roman tribune in the period following the death of Christ. In 1953 this was made into a very successful film that starred the young Welsh actor, Richard Burton.

Not forgotten
*But sporting events
severely curtailed*

The British addiction to sports of every kind was not forgotten during World War II, although it was severely curtailed. Following the declaration of war on Germany on 1 September 1939, it became necessary to assign many of London's leading sports grounds to other wartime purposes. Apart from the indignities noted earlier in this volume that were inflicted on the sports grounds of Wimbledon and Twickenham (see Nowhere Was Sacred), the test match ground known as the Oval at Kennington in South London, home to the Surrey County Cricket Club, was used as a prisoner-of-war camp.

London football clubs such as Arsenal and Queen's Park Rangers lost most of their players, as they joined the armed services and travel restrictions made it difficult for them to travel any distance to away matches. Eventually a London League was formed to replace the normal divisions. This was gradually expanded to include clubs such as Watford,

Aldershot, Portsmouth, Southampton and Brighton, whose players and spectators had reasonably good transport links to London. This development annoyed the chairman of Norwich City, who felt excluded and observed that spectators would be safer in Norwich than in London. His observation was true, but how would spectators travel there when the trains were full and the railway lines were likely to be bombed? Restrictions were also placed on the number of spectators allowed into each football ground to avoid any heavy casualties from bombing during a match.

Denis Compton

However, the Luftwaffe was more interested in attacking airfields and docks than disrupting the English football season. Besides, the local police often quietly ignored these restrictions.

Nevertheless, some precautions were taken. Greyhound and speedway racing, sports that traditionally took place in the evenings under lights, were discontinued. Furthermore, the roof of London's Wembley Stadium was painted black in an attempt to make it less conspicuous, although it continued to be used. On Saturday 10 May 1941, the stadium hosted the Cup Final. At this event, 60,000 spectators watched Arsenal draw 1-1 with Preston North End, the Arsenal goal scored (and a penalty missed) by Leslie Compton, brother of the famous cricketer Denis Compton, who also played for Arsenal.

Later the same evening the Luftwaffe arrived to deliver London the worst raid of the war, with the House of Commons and Westminster Abbey damaged and almost 1,500 Londoners killed. The devastation of the raid was exacerbated by the fact that the Thames was at low tide,

so it was hard for fire fighters to draw water to extinguish the flames. This turned out to be the last major raid of the Blitz, as the Luftwaffe subsequently turned east to fight the Russians. The following year, in more peaceful circumstances, a Cup Final crowd of 75,000 at Wembley saw Arsenal thrash Charlton Athletic 7-1, with Denis Compton appearing on the score sheet on this occasion.

The sacred turf of Lord's Cricket Ground in St John's Wood escaped conscription into the war effort. And even when Lord's was used as an RAF recruitment centre, the main pitch was preserved. However, the Luftwaffe was less respectful. When an oil bomb landed near the sightscreen and failed to explode, a photograph of a German officer fell out that bore the message 'With Compliments'. This just wasn't cricket! Presumably the officer wasn't hoping to become a member of the Marylebone Cricket Club.

Some cricket matches continued throughout the war, including the annual university match between Oxford and Cambridge. Some inter-services matches were also played,

with the RAF fielding distinguished
players such as the England batsmen
Cyril Washbrook and Bill Edrich
in 1941. In 1943 cricket matches
featured England Elevens, which saw
players as famous as Denis and Leslie
Compton, Trevor Bailey, Alec Bedser
and Leslie Ames playing against
Commonwealth teams with stars like
the Australian, Keith Miller, and the
West Indian, Learie Constantine (see
Making a Point).

By 1945, attendances at Lord's
were actually exceeding pre-war
levels. As the war drew to an end
in May, 100,000 people watched
Australia beat England in a three-
day game, a test match in all
but name.

ETIQUETTE SUSPENDED
*In 1942, the distinguished England
batsman and occasional opening
bowler Bill Edrich, a professional
cricketer, was watching a minor
cricket match. Edrich was in the
company of the amateurs Pelham
('Plum') Warner and G O ('Gubby')
Allen, both former England cricket
captains and of course amateurs, at a*

*time when no professional cricketer
would be chosen to lead his country.
Later the three had lunch together,
distinctions between amateur and
professional being in abeyance
during wartime.*

Not all heroes
Wartime proves profitable
for criminals

Not every member of London's
population proved to be a
hero during World War II. Some
took advantage of wartime blackouts
and other privations to engage in
highly profitable criminal activities.
'Mad' Frankie Fraser (1923–2014)
once explained that the war was such
a good time to be a criminal that
he never forgave the Germans for
surrendering.

Initially Fraser was an enforcer for
a gangster named Billy Hill. The latter
simply ignored his call-up papers,
instead embarking upon a series of
jewellery shop raids. One of these
raids resulted in an £11,000 haul
from New Bond Street – multiply
this amount by 25 for an idea of

present values. In June 1940 Hill was caught, following a raid on Hemmings of Conduit Street that put him in jail.

Fraser was nicknamed 'Mad' because he feigned mental illness to avoid conscription. His pursuit of a life of crime was interrupted only by the 42 years – accounting for more than half his adult life – he spent in prison. Fraser's speciality was razoring, but he also obliged his employers by removing people's teeth with pliers. Hill used him to deal with rival gangsters, and Fraser was allegedly paid by the stitch – so a cut requiring 25 stitches earned him £25.

Fraser was also a blackout looter, becoming one of a number of criminals who would arrive at the scene of an air raid in an 'ambulance' dressed in uniform, enter the ruined buildings, especially if they were shops, and emerge with stretchers carrying what appeared to be bodies covered with blankets. In fact, the 'bodies' were the possessions of the stricken business owners – although domestic dwellings also attracted these criminals if they were located in sufficiently prosperous areas.

Originally from Malta, the Messina brothers operated with more subtlety – and probably more profitably. At a time when many single young men were in the capital – including affluent Americans – as they waited to be sent into battle, the brothers supplied prostitutes. Besides being subjected to the usual threats from their pimps, these ladies were governed by certain strictly enforced rules: no bad language, no low-cut dresses, and not more than ten minutes per client. The Messina brothers prospered along these lines until the 1950s, at which point they were deported.

Others were even more violent than Frankie Fraser, who, as far as we know, never actually killed anyone. In June 1942, Cadet Gordon Cummins was hanged at Wandsworth prison, the only person to be hanged during an air raid. He had become known as the Blackout Ripper, having killed, and in some cases mutilated, four women, as well as attempting to murder two more. Despite overwhelming evidence, Cummins pleaded not guilty.

NOT QUITE BONNIE AND CLYDE

Two of the strangest and most incompetent criminals of the war period were the 22-year-old Karl Hulten, a Swedish-born deserter from the US army, and the 18-year-old Elizabeth Jones, a Welsh waitress. Hulten described himself as an officer and Chicago gangster – neither claim was true – while Jones wanted to be a stripper.

In October 1944 the couple met in a teashop, and over the next six days they committed a series of crimes in London: they robbed a nurse, tried to kill a hitchhiker, and murdered a London taxi driver. Leaving clues in their wake, Hulten was executed at Pentonville in 1945. Meanwhile Jones, who had confessed to the crimes, was reprieved, despite a campaign for her to hang; she was eventually released in 1954.

Valued allies
Poles make a significant contribution

Allied troops became a prominent feature of London life from the very first days of World War II. The Free French led by Charles de Gaulle, Belgians, Dutch, Czechs and Poles all settled in various communities either in or close to the capital. Many of the pilots who flew in the Battle of Britain were recruited from them, most conspicuous of which were the Poles.

Initially Sir Hugh Dowding, Commander-in-Chief of RAF Fighter Command, would not use men from these communities for battle, worried that language problems would lead to misunderstandings and 'friendly fire' accidents. However, when these men were eventually allowed to enter the battle their contribution was devastating. Their fanatical hatred of the Germans, who had invaded and devastated their countries, infused them with a ferocity and an indifference to risk that astonished their British commanders.

Number 303 Polish Fighter

Squadron was the most successful unit in Fighter Command, shooting down 126 German aircraft in 42 days. One of the pilots in the squadron, Czech Sergeant Josef František, was credited with 17 victories – this was the highest number of any pilot in the battle. It is therefore not surprising that the Polish and Czech fighters were consistently the most popular among the Londoners, as well as the wider British public.

Rather ambiguous
British wartime attitude to her Russian allies

During World War II, Britain's relations with her Russian allies were a little more ambiguous than those she shared with her allies from France, Belgium, the Netherlands, Czechoslovakia and Poland (see Valued Allies). In August 1939 Hitler and Stalin had agreed to the Ribbentrop–Molotov Pact, which guaranteed that neither country would attack the other. Hitler then invaded Poland with Stalin's tacit agreement.

Following the line Stalin had taken by signing the Pact, the Communist Party of Great Britain also declared itself against the war, denouncing it as a capitalist plot. Not many of its fellow Britons agreed with the party, so few complained when

Hammer and sickle

its newspaper, *The Daily Worker*, was closed down. This spared the publication the embarrassment of being opposed to the war when Hitler invaded the Soviet Union in June 1941 – literally overnight, the British Communists became enthusiastic patriots.

Churchill also changed his attitude towards the Russians. Long an arch adversary of the Communist tyranny, when questioned about his attitude to providing Hitler's latest victim with help, Churchill replied: 'If Hitler were to invade Hell I should at least make a favourable reference to the devil in the House of Commons'. Ivan Maisky, the Soviet ambassador to Britain, had previously been shunned by his hosts. Yet a week after Hitler's attack on Russia, he reported that everyone was now pro-Russian – and that the collected speeches of Stalin and Molotov were flying off the bookshelves.

The Communist Party of Great Britain threw its weight behind efforts to help the country's new ally, urging workers to greater feats in the production of tanks, guns and anything else that could be sent to Russia to help its defence. In the spring of 1942, George Orwell approvingly commented that an enormous hammer and sickle flag was flying over Selfridges in London, the store being a symbol of the capitalism he disdained. Yet he added that many working people did not associate Communism with Russia.

Generally speaking, it can be concluded that the people of London and Britain as a whole deplored Communism, but applauded the Russian war effort. The British support for the Russian people was clearly expressed in the Sword of Stalingrad, a magnificent 1m (4ft)-long weapon made of the finest steel and forged by the Wilkinson Sword company. Commissioned by King George VI, no effort was spared in its design and manufacture – indeed, it was decorated with rubies, gold and silver. Sir Ellis Minns, an expert in Slavonic iconography and President of Pembroke College, Cambridge devised the sword's Russian inscriptions, which translate: 'To the steel-hearted citizens of Stalingrad; the gift of King George VI; in token of the homage of the British people'.

The Sword of Stalingrad was exhibited throughout Britain, where many thousands queued to see it, before it was taken to the Tehran Conference in November 1943, where Churchill presented it to Stalin. The sword is now on display at the museum of the Battle of Stalingrad in the city whose heroic defence it commemorates – Stalingrad's name was changed to

Volgograd following the revelation of Stalin's crimes in the 1950s.

SWORD OF HONOUR

The Sword of Stalingrad features in the final volume of Evelyn Waugh's wartime trilogy, **Unconditional Surrender,** *as well as giving its name to the title of the trilogy:* **Sword of Honour.** *The principal character* **Guy Crouchback,** *disillusioned with the war and what he sees as his country's shameful alliance with a godless Communist tyranny, passes the queues waiting to see the sword in Westminster Abbey. Meanwhile, the sinister Corporal-Major Ludovic has no such inhibitions: he visits the abbey in the hope of gathering material for his volume of* **Pensées,** *which will eventually make his fortune and enable him to buy Crouchback's Italian home, Castello Crouchback. Since Crouchback is a man of honour and Ludovic a pretentious charlatan – and quite possibly a murderer – the reader is left in no doubt as to Waugh's feelings about the sword and all it represents.*

Little America
US troops 'overpaid, oversexed and over here'

The relationship between Londoners and their most important allies, the troops of the USA, turned out to be the most complex of all. President Roosevelt, who recognized from the outset of the war the need to support Britain – Europe's only remaining major democracy – at first was strongly opposed by many of his compatriots. Indeed, the USA avoided direct involvement in the conflict until Japan attacked their naval base at Pearl Harbor in Hawaii on 7 December 1941. At that point, to the relief of both Roosevelt and Churchill, Hitler obligingly declared war on the USA.

Nevertheless, there was much resentment among Londoners and the British that the USA had stayed out of the conflict in 1940, during the time of Britain's greatest peril. This was reflected in their attitude to the US troops who began to arrive in Britain in 1942 – but this resentment was less than fair. Already the USA had compromised its neutrality

Bundles for Britain

during the early stages of the war to provide naval vessels and armaments under what were known as lend-lease arrangements. In addition, many private citizens had sent food parcels and what were known as Bundles for Britain, consisting of clothing. American blood donors had also contributed substantial quantities of blood plasma, all these being sent in convoys across the Atlantic during the Blitz.

However, resentment was further compounded by the fact that US soldiers in Britain suffered few of the privations that were already routine among Londoners and the rest of the British population. This was clearly reflected in the differences in pay, with an American private soldier being paid more than an RAF flight lieutenant. Since the uniforms of the American private soldiers resembled those of British officers, they were occasionally saluted in the street, causing further resentment. The forces of the USA also had more on which to spend their money, since with the Americans came provisions that were available in their own stores but not in British shops.

Hence native Londoners and British started to apply the expression 'overpaid, oversexed and over here' to the US troops. To which the Americans replied, the British were 'underpaid, undersexed and under Eisenhower', as the American general had been appointed as the supreme commander in Europe. The private soldiers became known as GIs, an expression originally derived from the abbreviation of galvanized iron, a material commonly used by the American logistics corps. Later GI was also used as an abbreviation for General Issue and Government Issue.

One of the most popular venues in London for the American soldiers was the club Rainbow Corner. Located on the corner of Denman Street and Shaftesbury Avenue, this occupied the site of a former Lyons restaurant (see Not Fine Dining).

Meanwhile, the US officers' mess could be found in the ballroom of Grosvenor House in Park Lane. General Dwight Eisenhower, the US commander, occupied rooms at the nearby Dorchester hotel, which was rumoured to be bombproof. Thus the area around Grosvenor Square became known as Little America, with Shepherd Market named Eisenhower Platz.

Nevertheless, the real action took place at the Rainbow Corner club, which was open 24 hours a day. In the foyer of the establishment, a signpost bore three signs that read: 'Leicester Square 100 yards'; 'Berlin 600 miles'; New York 3,271 miles'. There would congregate American soldiers, young women and spivs. The young women, some prostitutes but most not, were in search of American boyfriends who would take them to restaurants and buy them meals that were different from those on the ration, present them with gifts of nylon stockings, or lemonade, sweets and chewing gum for their younger siblings. Above all, these American boyfriends would take their girlfriends to dances where they

could perform new American dances like the Jitterbug, denounced as immoral by some commentators. And they would be able to hear the music of Benny Goodman and the Big Band of Glenn Miller, who played in London while he served as a member of the US forces.

At the very least, a visit to the area surrounding Rainbow Corner would enable these ladies to experience the delights of exotic and unfamiliar foods such as waffles, Dunkin' Donuts and coffee. Before the arrival of instant coffee, this beverage, for most

Dorchester hotel

English people, took the form of Camp Coffee, a Scottish product that was made from sugar, chicory and a very small amount of caffeine-free coffee.

In the late spring of 1944, most American troops made their way to the south coast of England en route to Normandy. Proprietors of pubs, restaurants and other places of entertainment missed them, as no doubt did the many ladies in search of nylons. However, they were probably not missed as much by the male population of London.

Before their departure there was one final alarm. A contingent of US troops was taken to West Ham United's football stadium at Upton Park. Here they were briefed on the invasion plans, issued with French money and told that, for security reasons, they would have to remain in the stadium until setting off for Normandy. The US troops subsequently rebelled, broke out of the stadium grounds, and spent a last night celebrating in the West End. Happily, there was no breach of security!

MYSTERIOUS DISAPPEARANCE

Glenn Miller (1904-44) was one of the leading exponents of the Big Band sound, which emerged in the 1930s USA. In the years leading up to World War II, he was the world's leading recording artist with tunes like 'Chattanooga Choo Choo', and his band featured in two Hollywood films. Despite being above the call-up age, Miller succeeded in being accepted into a post by the US forces. In 1944 he subsequently brought a 50-piece military band to London, which gave 800 performances in the capital and beyond, and made recordings at the famous Abbey Road studios.

Glen Miller

On 15 December 1944, Miller set out from Bedford, the venue for his last concert, to fly to Paris to play for troops there. Mysteriously, he was never seen again: during the flight, his plane disappeared over the English Channel. It has been suggested that Miller was either the victim of a faulty carburettor or of a tragic accident. Indeed, it is possible an Allied bomber, returning to base from an unsuccessful mission, had jettisoned its bombs that struck his plane. To add to the mystery, no trace of him or the plane has ever been found.

Knights errant
Tensions develop between US troops and Londoners

In World War II, many US troops were sent to the countryside in the west of England to train for the eventual invasion of Europe. When they arrived, they were often charmed by the textbook village scenes that greeted them, which they had previously only seen in Hollywood films. Since these villages were less likely to have been damaged by German bombing and food was more readily available from the nearby farms, these foreign troops were made more welcome here than in London. As a result of the devastation caused by the Blitz, in the capital the population was shabby and short of everything, and therefore resented the relative comfort enjoyed by their American allies (see Little America).

Indeed, some of the young Americans living in London during the war commented that they had never been invited to an English person's home. Meanwhile others said they felt like knights errant arriving to rescue a rather shabby maiden, whose reaction to their arrival had been to complain they were late. Some attempts were made by US commanders to prepare their troops for what they would find in Britain, as did films and guidebooks. If a member of the US forces was invited to an English home, he was instructed not to spread the week's butter ration on one slice of bread, and not to complain if the beer was warm. Moreover, it was explained that the word 'rubber' in England meant 'eraser' – and not, as in the USA, a contraceptive. Naturally, one or two misunderstandings arose over the latter delicate point!

George Orwell commented that anti-American feelings were common among all classes – apart from young adults, especially those with a technical education. In 1943 he wrote an article for *Tribune* that described the degree of hostility between Londoners and their American visitors, describing the capital as feeling like occupied territory in places. Drunkenness (not confined to American troops), differences in pay and delusions among the Londoners caused by watching American films all created a toxic mixture of jealousy and misunderstanding. Orwell also reported reciprocal hostility amongst the US troops. His own resentments may be discerned in the article for the left-wing journal, which brought a firm riposte from a resident of Salisbury in Wiltshire where, for the reasons noted above, the US troops were made more welcome.

SUPREME DIPLOMAT

US troops who committed crimes against British subjects were tried by their own tribunals, not by British courts. This procedure was agreed by the respective governments but not widely known – indeed, the newspapers did not draw attention to this potentially embarrassing fact. However General Eisenhower, the US commander, was well aware of the difficulties of the relationship between

Dwight Eisenhower

his own troops and the British.

*Always a supreme diplomat,
Eisenhower therefore relaxed this
rule on occasions, as in the case of
the murderer Karl Hulten (see Not
Quite Bonnie and Clyde). He also
informed his officers that, in the event
of inevitable disagreements between
British and American officers, it was
perfectly in order to call one's British
adversary by the traditional American
expletive 'sonofabitch'. Yet he added
that anyone using the expression
'British sonofabitch' would find
himself in trouble.*

Question of colour
*Black US troops are welcomed
in London*

Knowing of the racial segregation
that disfigured many states of
the USA, Anthony Eden, the British
Foreign Secretary, suggested to
General George Marshall, Roosevelt's
Secretary of State and Chief of Staff
of the United States Army, that
during World War II no black soldiers
should be sent to Britain, which
had very different attitudes towards

matters of race. Many Britons warmly
remembered the black citizens
from the Commonwealth who had
travelled to what they regarded as
the mother country at the outbreak
of war, long before the Americans
arrived, to serve both in the armed
and civilian defence services. More
than 15,000 arrived from the West
Indies alone, many working in
munitions factories and the RAF,
while in parts of London, notably St
Pancras, they also served as air raid
wardens and auxiliary firemen.

Marshall told Eden that this request
was impractical, given the large
number of US servicemen who were
black. But as it turned out Eden was
right to be apprehensive, as difficulties
soon emerged. Black American
soldiers were popular with the British
population, who were particularly
impressed by their formation
marching without shouted orders – a
combination of military discipline
and rhythms of the dance hall, where
black-inspired jazz was becoming
popular. Moreover, some British
women were more than happy to be
accompanied to dance halls by black
soldiers. The impeccable manners of

these servicemen no doubt reflected the knowledge that such liaisons would have been unthinkable even in cosmopolitan New York, let alone the Southern States where the Ku Klux Klan still thrived. Indeed George Orwell, in one of his acerbic comments on the visitors from the USA, claimed that the black soldiers were the only ones from the US with really good manners. Children particularly liked the black soldiers, who gave them sweets.

White American soldiers were unimpressed with this state of affairs, complaining that the British girls went out with their fellow citizens who were regarded as 'American Indians' – this strange expression may have owed something to the presence in London of Sikh regiments from India. Thus several embarrassing incidents followed involving black members of the US forces. In October 1942 Lord Salisbury, Secretary of State for Dominion Affairs in the wartime government, reported that a black civil servant from the Colonial Office had been refused a table in a restaurant. This was because the restaurant manager was afraid that it would offend and deter the US officers from eating there, whose custom he valued. Upon being told this Churchill, with more wit than taste, replied 'That's all right. If he takes a banjo with him they'll think he's one of the band'.

GI BRIDES

Inevitably, there were romances between US soldiers and British women. Thus in 1946 the United States Army's movement dubbed Operation War Bride began transporting 70,000 women, and some children, to a new life in the USA. They qualified for free passages, which the US government paid for. To marry his British sweetheart, an American serviceman had to obtain the permission of his commanding officer. This was almost always granted if the serviceman and his bride were both white. However, it was refused if the serviceman was black and the bride white, as inter-racial marriage was still forbidden in some US states.

Making a point
Constantine's high profile race case

The great West Indian cricketer Learie Constantine (1901–71), later Baron Constantine, worked as a welfare officer in Liverpool during World War II. Here he played in the Lancashire Cricket League, where one of his tasks was to arrange fund-raising cricket matches for wartime charities. Thus in July 1943 he travelled to London to play some charity matches, booking rooms for four nights at a hotel in Russell Square for himself, his wife and their young daughter.

On the family's arrival, the hotel receptionist was less than welcoming. When Constantine asked to see the hotel manager, he was told 'You can stop tonight but not any longer' – it was explained that his presence would offend American visitors and could lead to disturbances. When Constantine's superior at the Ministry of Labour was called and objected on Constantine's behalf, he was duly informed 'He can stay tonight but he has to leave tomorrow morning and if he doesn't his luggage will be put outside and his door locked'. Constantine subsequently moved to the nearby Bedford Hotel, where he was made welcome.

However, the matter didn't end there, because the eminent King's Counsel Sir Patrick Hastings took up Constantine's case. It was raised in the House of Commons where the Home Secretary, Herbert Morrison, was sympathetic to Constantine's situation, a view expressed with caution as the case was still *sub judice*. The judge, Justice Birkett, decided in Constantine's favour, commending the cricketer for bearing himself with 'modesty and dignity' and rejecting the hotel manager's arguments that she had not been offensive.

Learie Constantine

Justice Birkett regretted the fact that, owing to the nature of the law in the matter, he could only impose a penalty of 5 guineas (£125 at today's value) instead of the exemplary damages requested. But a point had been made, the case was widely reported, and Constantine received hundreds of sympathetic letters from correspondents, many of whom were admirers of his cricketing achievements.

Sadly, this high profile case didn't solve the problem of racial tensions. In August 1944, George Orwell reported that a black British sergeant of the Home Guard had been refused entry to a dance hall for fear of upsetting American guests. Meanwhile, a report of a 'color bar' in another such establishment brought forth a confusing statement to the effect that there had never been a 'color bar', and that if there ever had been, then there no longer was!

Sheer necessity
Women needed, but not on equal terms!

First observed in World War I, the acceptance of women into roles

Female factory worker

traditionally undertaken by men gathered pace during World War II through sheer necessity. More women than ever before were employed in both industrial jobs and the services. Yet in the case of essential armaments production, women were rarely paid as well as men, despite the example set by the London Underground in World War I (see Preferable to Hobbledehoys).

Nevertheless, by the end of the war women accounted for more than a quarter of the British industrial workforce. They were manufacturing as well as assembling components, lathe operating being one task to which women were particularly assigned. During the early part of World War II, these women were all volunteers. However, the National Service Act of 1941 enabled the government to conscript unmarried women between the ages of 20 and 30 into industrial or military occupations.

In some of these occupations the proportion of women was far higher, reaching 38 per cent in engineering, chemicals, shipbuilding and munitions, and 40 per cent in the manufacture of military aircraft and vehicles. Around 85 per cent of the women were in skilled or semi-skilled operations, with special courses laid on at many institutions specifically to train them for this work – East Ham Technical College in London was one of the busiest training centres.

Women were frequently employed in making munitions, a task that required a delicate touch. However, not all women completed their war work in factories – sometimes the work was on a very small scale.

Thus the Hulton collection of pictures contains a photograph of ten women in what is obviously a very comfortable home in the impeccably middleclass Surbiton in Surrey. These women are sitting around tables intent on what, at first sight, appears to be knitting. Except that the 'wool' they are handling is, in fact, electrical cabling, which they are turning into fuses for munitions.

SPEEDY CONSTRUCTION

In the early summer of 1943 (the exact date is lost), a film was made at a Vickers–Armstrong factory that showed the construction of a Wellington bomber in less than 24 hours from scratch. So just 21 hours and 15 minutes after the construction process started, the plane took off, the pilot having been awoken from his sleep and summoned to the works. Most of the factory's workforce were women – former domestic servants, nurses and seamstresses, the last group being particularly valued, as they had to stitch the linen fabric on to the frame of the bomber. The film of this extraordinary feat was shown in cinemas and widely publicized to convey to the Germans – and the Americans – just how determined the British population was to provide their armed forces with the war supplies they needed.

In uniform
Women join the armed services

About 100,000 women joined the British armed services during World War I, doing clerical and administrative work, but during World War II this number reached half a million. Members of the Women's Royal Naval Service, known as Wrens, worked at administrative tasks, but also maintained ships when they were in port for re-fitting or repair. In addition, Wrens were extensively involved in planning the naval operation for D-Day, with a total of about 100,000 women serving during the conflict.

Meanwhile, the Women's Auxiliary Air Service (WAAF) was created as war approached in July 1939. Members of the WAAF maintained and operated the network of barrage balloons that were tethered over cities to obstruct enemy aircraft, and also liaised with the Royal Observer Corps (ROC). In the latter, the WAAF worked in conjunction with Sir Hugh Dowding's Chain Home radar installations to spot oncoming aircraft.

Once spotted, the WAAF would report the numbers, types and heights of the attacking force to the operations rooms – notably at RAF Uxbridge from which Air Vice-Marshal Keith Park directed the

Members of the WAAF

defence of London and the South East. Their messages would be received by other WAAFs, who would plot the movement of enemy bombers on a map, thus enabling Park to deploy his own fighters to meet them as they approached the capital.

The activities of these young ladies of the WAAF were memorably depicted in the film *Battle of Britain* (1969). Dowding watched the premier of this film shortly before his death, pronouncing it to be as he remembered the battle. Eventually almost 200,000 women worked as WAAFs – the Uxbridge bunker is now a museum.

IDLE WOMEN

One of the more unusual tasks undertaken by women during World War II was that of crewing the canal boats that carried coal and similarly bulky cargoes along the inland waterways of Britain. These ladies wore badges that bore the letters IW, for Inland Waterways, and hence became known as Idle Women.

Susan Wolfit, wife of the actor Donald Wolfit, left an account of the time she spent sharing the tiny cabin of a narrowboat with two other women, as they carried coal between the Coventry coalfields and Limehouse basin in London during the later stages of the war. After two trips under the supervision of an experienced boatman, the female crew was left to fend for itself, delivering coal to companies like Heinz, Glaxo and Nestlé.

Female members of the narrowboat crews were paid £3 a week – considerably more than most women working in factories, who earned little more than £2 a week. However, even £2 a week was more than a woman would have earned as a housemaid before the war.

Khaki brigade
Women contribute to the ATS

The majority of women conscripted to the British armed services during World War II were in the Auxiliary Territorial Service (ATS). This was despite the fact that the ATS was actually a less popular choice among women than the other services because its khaki uniform was regarded as less attractive than the dark blue of the Wrens and the Air Force blue of the WAAFs.

The first female recruits to the ATS were employed as cooks, clerks and telephonists. Three hundred of these initial recruits accompanied the Army's British Expeditionary Force to France at the beginning of the war and were among the last to leave Dunkirk. By the end of World War II, more than 200,000 women belonged to the ATS, holding ranks up to that of chief controller, the equivalent of major general.

As men were needed to fulfil more combat roles, women in the ATS were gradually introduced to tasks such as driving trucks, as well as running searchlight and anti-aircraft batteries. Indeed, one searchlight regiment in London consisted entirely of women. As a result, some men expressed their amazement that these women were not only very competent at this searchlight work, but were also adept at tracking aircraft for anti-aircraft batteries – this was despite their supposedly excitable

natures and lack of interest in aircraft! At the same time, Churchill decreed that women should not be allowed to actually fire the guns, lest they become upset at having killed someone.

As planning for the invasion of Normandy proceeded in 1944, many women were employed in interpreting aerial photographs of the French coast. This enabled models to be constructed of the features and obstacles that the troops would

Mary Churchill and her father, Winston

encounter as they went ashore on the D-Day beaches. A few weeks later, women in the ATS searched further aerial shots for evidence of the launch sites used by the Germans for the V-1 and V-2 rockets so steps could be taken to destroy them. Two members of the ATS were rather well known: Mary Churchill, the youngest daughter of the Prime Minister, accompanied her father when he visited the searchlight battery she commanded in London; meanwhile Princess Elizabeth served in London as a qualified mechanic and qualified as a driver of army vehicles.

Monty

MONTY STUMBLES

During World War II, visits to factories by leading military figures across London and the rest of Britain were organized to raise morale, with General Bernard Montgomery (1887–1976) being a favourite choice. Nicknamed 'Monty', he revelled in this work and was very good at it, although on a visit to one factory he came close to committing a **faux pas.**

Having assured his listeners that

Britain would win the war, he told them that it was because 'we've got the best men,' hurriedly adding, 'and the best women too of course.' Wild cheering followed. However, despite the preponderance of women in skilled operations in the engineering industries, few were paid the same rate as men doing identical work. The idea that women didn't really need to work or did it for pin money died hard.

Valiant warriors
Home Guard defends the capital

Since World War II, the Home Guard has been immortalized in the timeless BBC series *Dad's Army*. This popular comedy features the valiant, if often hapless, warriors of the fictional Walmington-on-Sea Home Guard, whose many conflicts with Chief Air Raid Warden Hodges prepared them for anything that Hitler could possibly have thrown at them.

Meanwhile, the real Home Guard was first mentioned during a broadcast made by Anthony Eden, Secretary of State for War, on the evening of 14 May 1940, four days after the Germans invaded Western Europe. Eden called upon men from the age of 17 to 65 to become Local Defence Volunteers, a title that was swiftly changed to Home Guard by Churchill. By July 1940 approximately 1½ million men had volunteered for this new organization.

Those who joined or remember the Home Guard from their younger days confess that many episodes of *Dad's Army* contain incidents that strike a familiar, if embarrassing, note. Yet on the third anniversary of the Home Guard's formation in May 1943, George Orwell, normally an acerbic critic, wrote of the defence organization with admiration and affection.

Eden's call drew an enthusiastic response from London, with Home Guard units often associated with companies or government organizations. Thus the Southern and London Midland railway companies formed units based at Waterloo and Euston, the former using a converted coach as its headquarters. Then a London taxi driver Home Guard unit ferried other units to Epping Forest to resist attacks from a unit supposedly advancing from Southend.

A City firm set up a shooting range on its roof and a women's Home Guard unit, based in Leicester Square, received instruction on marksmanship from the Labour MP Dr Edith Summerskill, herself a very skilled shot. Meanwhile, the London Gun Club opened its depot at Northolt to units and members of the public who needed firearms training. The

Member of the Home Guard

London County Council at County Hall formed its own unit, while across the river the Houses of Parliament also had its own unit consisting of Members, Peers and Parliamentary staff under the expert tuition of a sergeant of the Grenadier Guards.

By 1942, members of the Home Guard had Sten guns and small artillery pieces. They were taking over guard duties for prisoners of war and anti-aircraft defences from regular troops, and were integrated with the regular army and civil defence forces. Some had been trained to go undercover in the event of an invasion and conduct guerrilla warfare from behind enemy lines. Orwell observed that by 1943 2 million citizens could now be called to arms at short notice, and that the authorities could contemplate with satisfaction, rather than anxiety, the fact that these citizens had rifles in their bedrooms.

It is interesting to learn that not all Home Guard units were land bound. There was also a Home Guard River Patrol under the command of a rear admiral, which used their own boats, crewed by friends, to patrol the Thames in and around London.

RICH IRONY

Much early training of the Home Guard was based upon the practice of Tom Wintringham (1898–1949), an acquaintance of Orwell. An Oxford-educated avowed Marxist and active member of the Communist Party of Great Britain, he co-founded the party's newspaper **The Daily Worker** *then reported from Spain as its correspondent during the Spanish Civil War. Eventually he commanded the British Battalion of the International Brigade that fought against Franco in that conflict. On returning from Spain, he condemned the Communist Party's opposition to World War II and applied for an army commission, for which he was rejected.*

Wintringham subsequently opened his own Home Guard training school at Osterley Park mansion house in London, using his experiences from the war in Spain to teach members techniques of demolition, anti-tank combat, street fighting and guerrilla warfare. His work at Osterley was in time taken over by the government, yet by rich irony Wintringham was not allowed to join the Home Guard himself, owing to his Communist past! He unsuccessfully stood for Parliament then later became a film-maker, as well as a supporter of Marshal Tito's Yugoslavia against the tyranny of Stalin.

Amazing devices
Unusual weaponry of the Home Guard

Many devotees of the BBC comedy series *Dad's Army* will remember with special affection the improvised weaponry devised by the fictional Walmington-on-Sea Home Guard, the inventions usually belonging to Jack ('Don't Panic') Jones, the butcher. In reality, some of the devices used by local units of the actual Home Guard were not actually that far distant from the imaginings of Corporal Jones.

One of these was the Northover Projector, the anti-tank weapon designed by a Major Harry Northover, a Home Guard officer. This device consisted of a metal tube like a drainpipe that measured approximately 6cm (2½in) in diameter, which was mounted on a tripod that could itself be mounted on a cart or motorbike. Ammunition could include an ordinary hand grenade or a special incendiary grenade, the latter being a bottle filled with phosphorus. Propelled from the tube by lighting black gunpowder,

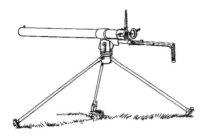

Northover Projector

the grenade would travel up to 274m (300yds). Upon hitting its target – or any intervening object – the bottle would explode in a cloud of flames and suffocating fumes. The accuracy of the Northover Projector, perhaps fortunately, was never tested in combat, although users reported it as being great fun to fire!

Then Colonel Tickler designed the Tickler Tank for the Maidenhead Home Guard. This amazing contraption consisted of sheets of scrapyard metal mounted on the chassis of a car. It is doubtful whether the armour of this self-styled tank would have resisted bullets, let alone shells, but no doubt local volunteers were cheered to know that they were now an 'armoured' platoon.

Finally, as an air defence measure there was the Z Battery, an anti-aircraft rocket that was essentially a far more sophisticated version of the Northover Projector. Developed in the 1930s for use by the Royal Navy – with the support of Churchill's favourite scientist Professor F A Lindemann – in this device cordite propelled a single rocket equipped with an explosive warhead.

The Z Battery was designed to bring down low-flying aircraft, but its accuracy was so poor that a second version, the ZZ, was developed to fire salvoes of rockets. This made a fearful noise – indeed, it was one of these that sparked the panic leading to the loss of life at Bethnal Green Underground station in March 1943 (see Tragic Postscript). Initially used by the regular army, both these batteries were transferred to the Home Guard from 1942 onwards.

As it turned out, the Home Guard rarely entered combat with the enemy. However, on one occasion a Home Guard unit based in London fired a volley of bullets at a low-flying German bomber that duly crashed. Cynics observed that two RAF fighters were also observed firing at the distressed aircraft at about the same time.

LIFEBUOY TOILET SOAP

Just as manufacturers of sweets, cigarettes and pre-digested cocoa tried to take advantage of rationing during World War II, so Lifebuoy Toilet Soap, manufactured by Lever brothers, associated its use with the Home Guard. A cartoon advertisement for the product featured a fictional Mr Ashby who, having returned from a hard day at the office, applied Lifebuoy soap to his perspiring body. This left him fit, energetic and presumably free of smell in order to set about his Home Guard duties 'like a youngster'. It is to be hoped that Mr Ashby did not use more than the 10cm (4in) of water that was recommended for baths during the war.

At ease, Home Guard
London prepares for peacetime

As the Allied armies advanced relentlessly across Europe towards the end of World War II, life in London began to assume a more peaceful character. On 30 October 1944, representatives of every unit of the London Home Guard gathered on Horse Guards Parade. They were addressed by Sir John Anderson, a member of the War Cabinet who had given his name to the shelters in their gardens now used for storing lawnmowers (see Cover At Home). During his address Anderson observed, with unintended irony, that it was as well the Home Guard had never been required to enter into action! In the months after this, the wartime civilian services, including the members of the Auxiliary Fire Service and the air raid wardens, followed them into retirement.

However, for members of the Home Guard post-war life was not the same as life had been before the great emergencies of 1940. For many, like the fictional Captain Mainwaring, Chief Warden Hodges and Corporal

Captain Mainwaring

creaking transport systems and shabby streets, which were still strewn with rubble from the Blitz, the doodlebugs and the rockets. The city was tired and battered, but proud, confident and determined as never before in her history.

Jones from the BBC series *Dad's Army*, it had been these men's finest hour, presenting them with a taste of authority and responsibility at a desperate time. Many members of the London Home Guard were dismissed from their last parade with regret. For many more, the experiences they had shared during the war years forged lasting friendships with people they would not have otherwise met, friendships that continued at home, in darts teams and at evenings spent reminiscing in the pub.

And so London, with a new Labour government, turned to the task of rebuilding its shattered homes,

INDEX

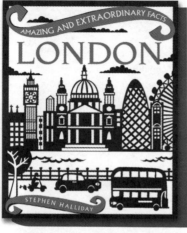

Amazing and Extraordinary
Facts: London
Stephen Halliday
ISBN: 978-1-910821-02-2

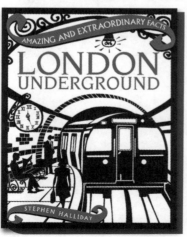

Amazing and Extraordinary
Facts: London Underground
Stephen Halliday
ISBN: 978-1-910821-03-9